The Daytona 500®

THE GREAT AMERICAN RACE™

The *DAYTONA* 500®

THE GREAT AMERICAN RACE™

DUANE FALK

MetroBooks

MetroBooks

An Imprint of the Michael Friedman Publishing Group, Inc.

Library of Congress Cataloging-in-Publication Data available upon request.

ISBN 1-58663-169-1

Editor: Nathaniel Marunas
Art Director: Kevin Ullrich
Designer: Mark Weinberg
Photography Editor: Lori Epstein
Production Director: Richela Fabian Morgan

Color separations by Radstock Repro
Printed in England by Butler & Tanner Ltd

10 9 8 7 6 5 4 3 2 1

For bulk purchases and special sales, please contact:
Michael Friedman Publishing Group, Inc.
Attention: Sales Department
230 Fifth Avenue
New York, NY 10001
212/685-6610 FAX 212/685-3916

Visit our website:
www.metrobooks.com

Dedication

To my wife, Cindy, with love

Acknowledgments

Many thanks to the folks at MetroBooks for their wonderful work on the book's layout and graphics, in particular Kevin and Lori. Thanks especially to Nathaniel, for his help in shaping the book and keeping it "on track." Thanks also to the folks at the Daytona International Speedway office and archives, and to Larry and others in the Living Legends of Racing group for their assistance on historical matters. Special thanks to Scott at Race Fan and to the folks at the local B&N stores, for their help in promoting my previous book and for their offer to do the same for this one! And, as always, thanks to my family for their patience, and to my friends (especially my coworkers at ISD) for their support and enthusiasm.

PREVIOUS PAGES: *There's excitement in the air around the Daytona International Speedway as drivers and spectators gear up for the big event. Here, a rainbow-colored blur is all the camera captures of the pack as it roars past during a Speed Weeks event, February 12, 1999.*

OPPOSITE: *Richard Petty hoists the trophy for the 1974 Daytona 500, February 17, 1974. That year's race was historic for many reasons, not least among them the fact that it was only 450 miles (720km) long, thanks to the oil embargo. It was also the first time in NASCAR history that a driver had won back-to-back Daytona 500s.*

FOLLOWING PAGES: *In the predawn light of race day, there is plenty of activity in the garage area at Daytona. Crews and maintenance personnel scurry around making last-minute adjustments to the vehicles and to the track itself to make sure everything is just so for the most highly anticipated race of the Winston Cup calendar.*

CONTENTS PAGE: *Mark Martin (No. 6), Terry Labonte (No. 5), and Ricky Craven (No. 32) race three-wide at Daytona, February 18, 2001. As NASCAR has become more and more mainstream, the number and variety of corporations interested in sponsoring race teams have steadily grown, as evidenced by Martin's Viagra car, courtesy of pharmaceutical giant Pfizer.*

CONTENTS

Introduction

IT'S CALLED THE GREAT AMERICAN RACE and with good reason. It's the premier event in that uniquely American form of motorsports: stock car racing. Today, the Daytona 500 is perhaps the best-known and most prestigious single automobile race in the world, eclipsing even the long-renowned Indianapolis 500 in popularity and visibility. Other races are longer, pay out a bigger purse, or seat more fans, but the Daytona 500 is—well, it's like the opening ceremonies of the Olympics and the climax of the Super Bowl combined.

What is it about this one race that makes it so special and draws such heightened attention to the sport? For racing fans, the Daytona 500 is a breath of spring after a long winter. It's the start of the NASCAR season (finally!) and the first glimpse of new cars and new drivers. Race teams put considerable effort throughout the winter months into preparations for the Daytona 500, so their performance in Florida is a measure by which they can judge their readiness for the season. A good qualifying run and a good finish buoys a team, giving them a sturdy foundation on which to build a championship season through the following weeks and months.

ABOVE: *Winner! Seen here on Valentine's Day, 1999, Jeff Gordon rests his hand on the Daytona 500 trophy after winning the Great American Race. As the Winston Cup roars into the new millennium, Gordon is following in the footsteps of the great Dale Earnhardt (who won his fourth championship at the age of thirty-four, while Gordon won his fourth at the age of thirty).*

LEFT: *Races on the beach were run along the narrow strip of firm sand that lay between the soft sand and the surf, with the "safe" limit on the water side of the course set off by markers. The markers also showed officials when the tide had come in so far that it was unsafe to race. More than one beach race was red-flagged before its time due to the tides.*

Racing's top names gathered in the smoke-filled Ebony Room atop Daytona Beach's Streamline Hotel to hammer out a set of rules for the new organization called NASCAR, a name coined that day by mechanic Red Vogt. The attendees bandied about several monikers for the organization, but other groups had already taken the other names.

The race and the racetrack also have the considerable weight of tradition and history behind them. NASCAR was born and bred in Daytona Beach, Florida, and NASCAR still maintains its headquarters there. NASCAR's top-level series is the Winston Cup. Today, it's schedule covers nineteen states and twenty-three tracks, but its heart and soul are on the sands of Daytona Beach, where the story of the Daytona 500 and NASCAR itself begins.

The Roots of NASCAR

There has been automobile racing in the United States ever since there were automobiles to race. In the early days, races featured special prototype vehicles, or factory models built especially for racing. Once the ownership of "family cars" reached sufficient saturation, though, it was inevitable that folks would start

racing those as well. All across rural America in the 1930s, rough dirt tracks were ploughed from farmers' fields where the local speedsters would gather on weekends to race their "modified" coupes. These gatherings were the roots of stock car racing.

The sport may well have stalled at that amateur level were it not for fortuitous circumstances in Daytona Beach in the late 1930s. Various stock car racing organizations had formed around the country, but none had the scope, authority, or prestige to organize beyond the local level and certainly not to raise the sport to national prominence. In 1934, a mechanic and racer from Washington, D.C., "Big Bill" France, who had relocated his family to Daytona Beach, Florida, became involved—first as a racer, then as a race organizer.

After World War II, which had put a hold on all forms of motorsports because of rationing, France decided to apply the lessons he'd learned as a race promoter and form a sanctioning body that would organize stock car racing. His guiding principles were: a clear set of rules that everyone would adhere to; a solid schedule of events with guaranteed payouts (many track promoters were notorious for skipping out after a race without paying the winnings); a championship based on points earned at each race; and cars that were *strictly stock*. The last point would guarantee broad participation, since racers could practically drive their family car right from the road onto the track and catch the attention and interest of fans, who could identify the cars on the track with the ones in their garages at home. The principles were appealing enough that France was able to attract the top talent of the day, with whose help he formed the National Association for Stock Car Automobile Racing (NASCAR) at the Streamline Hotel in Daytona Beach in 1947.

ABOVE: *NASCAR founder Bill France Sr. (left) and future steward Bill France Jr. on the beach. As superspeedways replaced dirt tracks on the circuit, the France family business expanded to include management of the Daytona and Talladega superspeedways (through the International Speedway Corp.).*

LEFT: *The Daytona beaches weren't just for racing. Not far from the racecourse the beaches featured boardwalks and bandshells and the summer homes of such luminaries as Ransom Olds and John D. Rockefeller.*

ABOVE: *H.T. Thomas was the pilot, Ransom Olds the owner. With Thomas at the wheel, The Pirate set an important speed record at Daytona Beach in 1903: 54.38 mph (87kph).*

RIGHT: *Barney Oldfield set speed records, too, but more importantly, he opened up auto racing to the working class. Unlike many of his aristocratic peers, Oldfield was the son of a poor farmer. His daring driving style proved that anyone could race cars. Oldfield retired from racing in 1918, but he continued to make public appearances and starred in such racing movies as* Blonde Comet *(1941).*

INTRODUCTION

Pioneers on the Beach

It was more than the sunny climate at Daytona Beach that attracted France when he moved south. There is an apocryphal story that France ended up at Daytona Beach because his car broke down there on his way farther down the coast. Given his mechanical aptitude, though, it's more likely that he stopped because he was attracted by the history of auto racing in the area.

Since the very beginning of the twentieth century, automotive pioneers had taken their creations to Daytona Beach to show them off and try for the coveted land speed record. Ransom E. Olds, progenitor of the Oldsmobile marque (i.e., trademark), was the one who started it off. While wintering at a hotel on nearby Ormond Beach, he discovered the long, smooth stretches of hard-packed sand and deemed them perfect for speed runs. In 1903, he set the first record there in his *Pirate*. Other thrill seekers and mechanical mavens soon joined him, and by 1910, there was an official "Speed Week" at Daytona.

The speeds on the beach climbed dramatically over the years, as the top talent in the sport took their machines there. Millionaire William Vanderbilt and veteran racer Barney Oldfield were among the early record breakers, with Oldfield's 1910 run exceeding 131 mph (210.8 kph). British racers Sir Malcolm Campbell and the "Mad Major," Sir Henry Seagrave, brought their fancifully-named *Bluebird* and *Golden Arrow* cars to challenge the record set by America's *Triplex Special*. Campbell

ABOVE: *Also known as the "Mad Major," Henry Seagrave was the first man to break the 200-mph (320-kph) barrier. He did it on Daytona Beach driving the Golden Arrow. The Sunbeam Special (pictured here) ran 203.79 mph (326.1kph). It was long before the days of wind tunnel testing, but Seagrave's designers obviously knew the value of streamlining in achieving stability and high speeds.*

ended up king of the hill, topping out at 276.82 mph (445.49kph) in 1935.

While the Daytona and Ormond beaches were ideal for the early runs, once the speeds approached 300 mph (480kph), the flaws in the terrain soon became apparent, then dangerous. The 1926 Indy 500 winner, Frank Lockhart, was among those who were killed, as the beaches became too short and too rough to support the high speeds. By 1936 another venue had been found, and the speed record setters turned to the Bonneville Salt Flats instead of Daytona Beach. Sir Malcolm exceeded the 300-mph mark there—something no one had managed at Daytona—in 1935.

Early Races

Over those years the community of Daytona Beach had come to value the reputation and attendant revenue of being a world-class racing location. When the speedsters headed west, the city fathers decided they would need to

LEFT: *Daytona Beach was well known across the country as a popular tourist spot, and the chauffeured sedans of the well-to-do crowded the beaches near the hotels and resorts throughout the winter season.*

BELOW: *There was racing at Daytona Beach even before the hard-packed sands became the top spot for speed record runs. Annual races at Ormond Beach were among the first such events in the country (along with the Long Island, New York, Vanderbilt Cup); winners of the races at Ormond were awarded the Sir Thomas Dewar Trophy.*

The Bonneville Salt Flats

IN THE 1930s, THE CUTTING EDGE for land speed records shifted from Daytona Beach to the salt flats of Utah. The Bonneville Salt Flats offered everything that enterprising speedsters could want. The dried bed of a prehistoric inland sea is 159 square miles (411.8km) of a hard layer of potash salt that is an ideal surface for high-speed runs. The speeds attained there have far exceeded those attained on the beaches in Florida.

Racing at Bonneville (named after Captain Benjamin Bonneville, sponsor of the first expedition to chart the area) started as far back as 1904, when William Randolph Hearst hired a bicyclist to cross the flats as a publicity stunt. Interest was renewed in the 1920s when Ab Jenkins, from Salt Lake City, bet the locals that his Studebaker could beat the train from Salt Lake to nearby Wendover. He won his bet by taking the shortcut across the flats!

Once it became clear in the 1930s that Daytona Beach could no longer support speed runs, attention shifted to Bonneville and the records began to accumulate. Ab Jenkins and his *Mormon Meteor* figured prominently in the early records. In 1938 John Cobb upped the ante to 350.07 mph (560.1kph), only to be overshadowed the very next day by Captain G.E.T. Eyston's 357.50-mph (572kph) run. Cobb regained the top spot the following year at 369.74 mph (591.6kph).

By the 1960s the vehicles run at Bonneville resembled rockets more than automobiles. In fact, speed runs were segregated to wheel-driven and jet-driven categories to accommodate the new technology. Craig

Breedlove became a household name as the first person to exceed 600 mph (960 kph) on wheels, and Gary Gabolich holds the current overall record with his 1970 run in the *Blue Flame* at 622.407 (995.9kph) mph.

At no other place is the cult of speed as holy. Each fall the Bonneville Speed Weeks, The World of Speed, and the Bonneville World Finals are held consecutively from August through October. The events feature entries in many categories and subcategories of vehicles—from rockets to cars and trucks to motorcycles. There's even a category for bicycles, which boasts a current record of more than 160 mph (256kph) set recently by a Dutch cyclist.

If you're content to observe, you can pick races on the long or short tracks (the long track is used for vehicles exceeding 200 mph [320kph]). The best place to watch is a couple miles out from the starting line where the vehicle will be up to full speed. You can even participate in a speed run if you're so inclined. For

a modest fee, a driver with a safety helmet and a number taped on his or her vehicle can make a run on the course. You definitely want to stay on the marked courses—the salt layer there is a rock-hard 6 feet (1.8m) thick. As the infamous Donner party found out (they were delayed at the flats when their wagons' wheels mired in the muck under the salt), the salt in a given location may be only a crust of inches over a thick mud that will swamp your vehicle.

ABOVE: *Speed is the main industry at Bonneville, Utah. Bonneville's claim to fame as the world's fastest racetrack has diminished in recent years as its speed records have been eclipsed. Andy Green holds the current record at 763.035 mph (1,220.9kph), set in 1997 in his Thrust SSC jet vehicle at Black Rock Desert, Nevada.*

RIGHT: *Big Bill France, seen here at Daytona Beach in Red Vogt's Ford coupe, wasn't a bad racer in his own right. France had raced in the Washington, D.C., area before moving to Daytona. France actually won one of the first beach races he organized, but he wisely passed the trophy on to the next highest finisher for propriety's sake.*

RIGHT: *Sig Haugdahl had been racing at Daytona Beach for years before being tapped to organize the 1936 stock car race. He's shown here in 1922 in a car featuring an engine taken from a military hydroplane.*

take a different tack to maintain Daytona Beach's place in the racing world.

They turned to veteran racer Sig Haugdahl. Haugdahl had won several IMCA (International Motor Contest Association, a Midwestern fairground racing series) titles in the late 1920s and early 1930s and had retired to Daytona Beach. He suggested an oval race using the beach as one of the straightaways and the parallel highway A-1-A as the other. The course would be unique and, if stock cars were used, could support a large starting field. The 1936 National Championship Beach and Road Race, as it was called, was run on a 3.2-mile (5.1km) course, determined by finding the easiest places to cut turns into the dunes between the beach and the highway. The original Daytona Beach racer, Ransom Olds, was on hand as the Grand Marshal for the event.

For various reasons, the event was not quite the success the city had hoped for, neither from a racing or business standpoint, and they decided not to repeat it. Instead, they tried motorbike racing on the same course. The bikes were better able to handle the sand, and nearly 20,000 spectators turned out to watch the successful endeavor. Daytona Beach turned to motorcycles as its claim to fame.

One of the drivers in the field for the 1936 auto race had been Bill France. France had seen the success of the motorbike race and thought he could make a better go of an auto race than Haugdahl had. France convinced the Elks Club to support another event in 1937. It was closer, but not quite there; it took one more try, sponsored by local restaurant owner Charlie Reese, to get the details down. France had the local highway maintenance crew spread clay through the sandy turns, to harden the surface and prevent the formation of the car-stopping ruts that had plagued previous events. He also paid particular care to policing access to the race by spectators. The course was not self-contained, as most racetracks are, but wide open on all sides. So, while decent crowds showed up for the earlier races, many of them watched the races from the side of the highway or along the beach—without buying a ticket. By judicious posting of "Careful–Snakes" signs in the brush and scrub around the inland side of the track, France was able to keep most of the fans on the paths, which had ticket turnstiles at the end.

It looked like things were finally clicking, and France organized several more beach races up to the start of America's involvement in World War II in 1941. After the war, France resumed promoting races at the beach but, as noted above, was also pulling the pieces together for his own stock car racing organization.

BELOW: *During a 200-mph (320kph) run in 1928, Frank Lockhart's* Stutz Black Hawk *flew out of control and crashed into the surf. He was rescued unhurt as his car swamped in the breakers, but just months later he lost his life in a second crash at the same locale.*

the very first, which was run on a 2.2-mile (3.5km) Daytona beach and road course.

With enough new Detroit iron on the streets by 1949, the Strictly Stock series took flight that year. It immediately surpassed both the Roadster and Modified divisions in popularity and has been the mainstay of NASCAR racing since. And Daytona Beach has been right there, part of every season. It wasn't the lead-off race in the 1949 schedule (competition by rival stock car organization NSCRA prompted NASCAR to make an unplanned showing in Charlotte, North Carolina, instead), but it was the second event, and Daytona races have been at or near the start of each season ever since.

The course used for the Strictly Stock race was longer—4.1 miles (6.6 km)—but it was basically the same one the racers had been running on since 1936. The flag stand was on Highway A-1-A, and the cars ran about two miles (3.2 km) south on that narrow stretch of asphalt. As they approached the south turn, they'd throw their cars into a slide and cross over through the cut in the dunes to the beach itself. The pack would run north along the beach for an equal distance. The trick to running on the beach was to find the right line between the loose sand near the dunes of the "infield" and the surf on the ocean side. The damp sand was hard-packed and the speediest (and safest) place to run. At the end of the beach straight, there was another cutback across to the highway. This was the north turn, where the largest grandstands were located and most spectators gathered. (Most of the old photos of the

NASCAR Runs the Daytona Beach and Road Course

NASCAR's first season of racing was 1948. The organization was formed with three divisions, Roadsters, Modifieds, and Strictly Stock, but due to shortages following the war, the Strictly Stock series wasn't run that first year. The Roadsters never caught on, but the Modified division ran forty-eight events and crowned a series champion. NASCAR's first champ was Robert "Red" Byron, a long-time racer and decorated World War II veteran. Byron won eleven races in 1948, including beach races were taken from a vantage point outside of the north turn.) Then the racers headed back down the highway to the start/finish line and around again.

Racers faced a unique variety of hazards on the Daytona beach and road course. Where else were races subject to a red flag due to the tides coming in and flooding the track? If drivers strayed too close to the surf, they could find themselves foundering or rolling their car in the water. Visibility on the beach side was almost nil as windshields were quickly coated with wet sand. The end of the beach straightaway was not marked in any way, so if a driver didn't see the cut of the north turn, he could end up driving alone up the empty beach. Most drivers used the line of fans along the beach to determine where to turn. When you ran out of fans, you cranked the wheel left. The highway side posed its own dangers. The road was barely wide enough for two cars, so passing was a white-knuckle adventure.

Red Byron continued his winning ways and took the first Strictly Stock checkered flag at the beach in July 1949. Byron was driving the No. 22 Oldsmobile fielded by the very successful car owner Raymond Parks, and started the race in second place. Fourth-place starter Joe Littlejohn had leapt to the lead at the green flag, but lost it to Gober Sosebee before the first lap was over. Sosebee held onto the lead for most of the race, but spun in the north turn on lap 34 and fell back to eighth place. Byron was close behind, darted into the lead, and stayed there to take the win, with Tim Flock finishing second. The Strictly Stock division was renamed the Grand National Championship after the 1949 season (which in turn became the Winston Cup after 1970). Byron almost took the 1950 race as well, but suffered transmission problems that

RIGHT: *The No. 9 Studebaker looks out of place among the coupes in this early Modified series race at the beach. As drivers exited the north turn, they powered out onto highway A-1-A, often bottlenecking the traffic at that point.*

OPPOSITE: *Action in the north turn. Race cars were half out of control as the drivers slid them through the sand in the turns at the Daytona beach and road course. So if a car got crossed up, it could be tough for the other drivers to avoid making contact with it. The turns were the slowest parts of the track, but that was where much of the action took place.*

RIGHT: *Imagine Dale Jarrett climbing out of the No. 88 car today in this racing outfit. Safety rules were pretty casual in the early days of the sport: a helmet and goggles were about all the protective gear that was required in NASCAR's first decade. Fonty Flock dressed for a day at the beach in this photo, taken just before a race in the early 1950s.*

forced a pit stop and repairs halfway through. Harold Kite took over the lead and hung on to win in his very first Grand National start.

In 1951, the Hudson Motor Car Company produced a new model, the Hornet. The model proved to be ideal for racing. It had a low center of gravity that gave it better handling through corners than most other makes. Hudsons dominated the circuit for the next several years. Hometown hero Marshall Teague (in his No. 6 Fabulous Hudson Hornet) handily won the 1951 and 1952 Daytona races.

"Fonty" (short for Truman Fontello) Flock had the 1953 race in hand until his tank ran dry on the last lap. He got a push to the pits and refueled, but lost the lead to Bill Blair and finished second. One of Fonty's brothers, Tim (brother Bob and sister Ethel were the other Flock siblings racing in NASCAR), took the

INTRODUCTION

PREVIOUS PAGES: *This infield shot of the 1957 Daytona Beach-Road Course race shows that, while facilities were primitive at best, there was plenty of room on the sand for the crowds around and in the center of the course. Cotton Owens won the race in a Pontiac, the first Grand National victory for both man and marque.*

checkered flag in the 1954 event, but was later disqualified for what appeared to be carburetor modifications. Flock contested that the parts were stock, although to no avail. Angry over what appeared to him to be an arbitrary ruling, he quit the NASCAR circuit and sat out the rest of the season.

Tim Flock was back in full force for the 1955 Daytona race, though, hooking up with Wisconsin manufacturer Carl Kiekhafer.

Kiekhafer used a very methodical and scientific approach to racing (as he did with any endeavor he undertook) and took NASCAR by storm through the 1955 and 1956 seasons. Flock and Kiekhafer won eighteen races and the championship together in 1955, including the Daytona race. Flock won the 1956 beach race as well, but parted company with the team owner partway through that season. Kiekhafer provided his drivers with the very

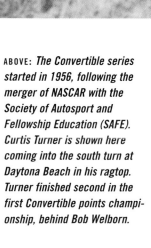

RIGHT: *Curtis Turner's 1956 Ford at Daytona Beach. Turner only ran thirteen out of forty-eight races in 1956, with one win. Turner started in the back of the pack and finished well down at the beach and road course that year. His fifty-second-place finish didn't even pay any consolation money for the effort.*

OPPOSITE INSET: *Junior Johnson was the model of a stock car racer in the 1950s. A former moonshine runner, Johnson took his driving talents to the track in 1953 and won fifty events in his career. He's shown here after a 1958 win (one of six for him that year) with Paul Spaulding's No. 11 Ford.*

ABOVE: *Curtis Turner was a daring racer and dashing entrepreneur. He enjoyed his greatest success in 1950 and '51 driving the No. 41 for John Eanes. "Pops" Turner lost his life in the crash of his personal plane in 1970.*

challengers. Successful Modified racer (in one season he'd won twenty-four straight events) and later ace car owner and mechanic Cotton (Everett) Owens took Pontiac to victory lane for the first time in NASCAR history. It was also the first of Owens's nine Grand National wins and came after a hard-fought duel with sophomore driver Paul Goldsmith.

Goldsmith drove a Pontiac at Daytona Beach the next year, owned and prepped by legendary mechanic Smokey Yunick. Goldsmith took an early lead, but spent the second half of the race fending off the hard-charging Curtis Turner. As the two dueled on the beach, Turner spun into the surf trying to avoid a slower car. Goldsmith opened up a ten-second lead, but lost it again when, on the last lap, he misjudged the cut to the north turn, and drove off course along the beach. He quickly caught his mistake and did a 180° to roar back onto the track. The damage was done, though, and Turner had closed to within striking distance. Yunick's stout power plant gave Goldsmith the edge he needed to hang on, and he took the checkered flag with a five car-length margin—the closest finish ever on the course.

best equipment but was also extremely demanding of them, and often eccentric in how he ran his teams. Despite their winning record, Flock found himself developing stomach ulcers from the tensions within the team, so he departed.

After the 1956 season, Kiekhafer departed NASCAR as suddenly as he'd arrived, leaving the 1957 Daytona race wide open to other

A Greater Vision

While the Daytona Beach races were popular with fans and were signature events in the NASCAR seasons, Bill France realized that the unique course had limited life remaining in it. By the mid-1950s, development along the beaches was beginning to encroach on the area, and the beaches themselves were deteriorating from the hard use. Due to the temporary nature of the track, there was also no good way to expand the all-important facilities for fans and race teams.

Despite enticement by other locales to relocate the popular event, Bill France was determined to keep NASCAR racing in the Daytona Beach area, and as early as 1950 began looking for a site for a permanent race facility. France convinced the local politicians of the continuing value of the program and was able to engage their assistance in raising funds and tracking down a site. By 1954, they'd secured a parcel of land near the Daytona airport and France announced that the Daytona Beach-Road Course (as it was then called) would host the 1955 race.

France's vision was for a superspeedway. At 1.366 miles (2.198km), Darlington Raceway was the largest paved track on the NASCAR circuit at the time, and that track stood out sharply from the half-mile (.8km) dirt tracks that made up most of the series events. But France was looking to the sport's future and envisioned an amazing 2.5-mile (4-km) track. There were few others who shared his far-

sightedness, though, and bureaucratic red tape was one obstacle that even the iron-willed France could not easily overcome. The speedway project was delayed again and again as commissioners hemmed and hawed, reviewing different alternatives. As the second half of the 1950s went by, it looked like "France's Folly" really was just a pipe dream.

The limitations of the beach course became more apparent each year, however, and the Daytona Speedway District Commission (as the

ABOVE: *The facilities for fans were almost nonexistent at the beach course. Even so, the 1957 race (shown here) drew 37,000 spectators. Cotton Owens was the winner, in the first NASCAR event to feature an average speed in excess of 100 mph (160kph).*

civic group responsible for the decision was called) was finally swayed by France's arguments. In 1957, the land was leased to the Daytona International Speedway Corporation, and Bill France was off to the races.

Most of the tracks at that time were makeshift affairs; even Darlington was laid out without any engineering assistance (hence the difference in banking and radius in each of its corners). Daytona would be different. France knew what he wanted from this track and had it designed to fit those specifications. First, it had to be fast: A 2.5-mile (4-km) paved track with high-banked turns would support speeds higher than anything NASCAR had yet run. Second, it had to be fan-friendly: There was plenty of extra room around the track for parking and other facilities, and plenty of room for grandstands. Charles Moneypenny offered his services in racetrack design and came up with a tri-oval configuration. The long, curved front straight allowed more room for stands, and gave fans all along that stretch of track a clear view of the entire arc. Construction on the (renamed) Daytona International Speedway began early in 1958, and it was again announced that that year's beach and road course race would be the last. This time, the race organizers were right.

BELOW: *As rough and tumble as the early days of NASCAR were, there were more women who participated in the sport at that time than ever since. Louise Smith was in at the very beginning, as a car owner and as a racer in the first Strictly Stock event at Daytona Beach.*

Daytona in the Early 1950s— A Firsthand Account

THERE AREN'T TOO MANY FOLKS AROUND now who were part of the early days at Daytona, but long-time racer Larry Shurter was able to provide a firsthand perspective on running at the beach.

Shurter, a native of the Catskill region of New York, had been running midget racers since 1938. How did he get his start in racing? A familiar story: "I was crazy as hell on the highway so when they opened the track in Woodstock thought I'd better take to the track there." After World War II he started appearing on the Midget racing circuit full-time. When he got a notice for the 1950 Daytona Beach race, he drove the family car, a 1949 Ford, down to Florida to try his hand at the stock cars.

"I didn't do too good in that one—I wasn't familiar with the bigger cars and probably drove too conservatively." His day ended when he ran up on "some young kids" who'd gotten crossed up in the south turn, and he finished twenty-fifth.

He made another run at the course in 1952, driving his partner's 1950 Oldsmobile. "I went down to the beach a couple of nights ahead to practice—it was probably illegal—but I was more ready for that race." He also picked out a landmark— a particularly tall palm tree—to use as a marker for the north turn, noting that "the sand was so bad you couldn't see anything. When I came up on that tree I knew to throw it into a slide for the turn." Shurter recalls running as high as fourth place before sand

worked into the shifter on his steering column and fouled the mechanism. "I got it into high and didn't dare take it out, but I couldn't get any speed out of the turns that way." He finished a respectable twelfth and earned all of $50.

Shurter also raced three other Grand National events in 1952, including a race at Pennsylvania's tough Langhorne track, but said that it was particularly tough for "fellows from above the Mason-Dixon line" to make a mark in NASCAR at that time. He continued to race Midgets and Modifieds in the northeast (including a run as track champ in Rhinebeck, New York), along with managing his family's sawmill and a local tavern.

Shurter has maintained a collection of photos and memorabilia from throughout his racing career and is active in the Living Legends of Auto Racing (LLOAR) organization. He still enjoys watching and attending NASCAR races. How do the drivers of today compare with the old-timers? "There's no comparison. Let's just say that they're not as crazy now! Turner, Weatherly… those fellows were real daredevils."

Chapter One

THE FIRST SUPERSPEEDWAY

PEOPLE TEND TO VIEW THE FUTURE through the lens of what they already know—more of the same, but bigger, better, faster, and cheaper. So the future of NASCAR in the late 1950s, in most minds, might have included one-mile (1.6-km) paved tracks instead of quarter-mile (.4 km) dirt rings, and better facilities, like more stands and maybe a garage for the teams. And, of course, bigger purses for the field. When teams first filed through the tunnel into the infield at Daytona, they were presented with something completely outside of their experience, and most didn't know what to make of it.

Even today, as familiar as we are with massive sports arenas and big tracks, most folks have the same reaction when they see Daytona International Speedway firsthand: "Wow—this place is

ABOVE: *"Little" Joe Weatherly was one of the first drivers to unravel some of the practical mysteries of aerodynamics, in particular applying his wisdom to "drafting" on the new superspeedways. It helped him to three top-five finishes in five Daytona 500 starts.*

LEFT: *Smokey Yunick is easy to pick out in any photo—just look for the distinctive hat. When Curtis Turner made his NASCAR comeback in 1966, he turned to Yunick to provide him with fast cars. The No. 13 crew services Turner here in the 1967 Daytona 500. Yunick remained active in the sport up until his death in 2001.*

HUGE!" Every statistic is larger than life. All around, the track is 40 feet (12.2m) wide, with an apron around the bottom between 12 and 30 feet (3.6m and 9.1m, respectively) wide. It's not the widest by today's standards, but the layout allows cars to use not just one or two grooves, but the whole width of the track for racing. The backstretch is straight and banked only enough to drain water and is 3,000 feet (914.4m) long. The turns at each end of the track are 3,000 feet long as well. The banking there is 31°—the

steepest angle they could manage with the asphalt-laying equipment of the time. That banking is so high that the track is actually three or four stories tall in the turns. The front stretch is a broad, flat arc 3,800 feet (1,158.2m) long. The pit road cuts across that arc, with the entrance off of turn four and the exit in turn one. It's 1,600 feet (487.6m) long, which is plenty of room to service a field of forty-three cars. There are some grandstands along the back straightaway, but most of the seating is along the front chute. If you're visiting Daytona, bring your binoculars, because the cars running down the backstretch are almost a half mile (0.8km) away

from the main grandstands! That translates to a 180-acre (72.8ha) infield, which holds seven different garages with space for 162 cars, a road course, and a 44-acre (17.8ha) man-made lake, Lake Lloyd. Vehicles enter and exit the infield via a tunnel under turn four.

As construction on the track neared completion at the end of 1958, car owners, drivers, media, and manufacturers' representatives were invited to see the project. There was considerable excitement among the crowd when they first came to visit the track. The facility was ordained the "Hollywood" of racetracks and called a "revolution in motorsports." After his initial visit, driver Marvin Panch decided to postpone his planned retirement in order to have a run at the new track.

There was some trepidation as well, though. According to driver Jimmy Thompson, "There have been other tracks that separated the men from the boys. This track will separate the brave from the weak, after the boys are gone." Plainspoken Lee Petty laid it out in an interview after the first race: "We were all rookies going thirty to forty miles an hour faster than we ever had before. There were some scared cats out there!" Opinions were mixed prior to the race as to whether the cars, the tires, and the drivers could hold up for 500 miles (804.6km, the announced length of the event) at the speeds the track could support. A tragic and fatal crash at the track the week before the first big race certainly didn't help dispel the concerns.

The First Daytona 500: 1959

What had been Speed Week at Daytona turned into two weeks of activity at the new track. Qualifying events occurred over the two weeks prior to the main attraction. The

qualifying routine for Daytona was different than that at most other tracks. Four time-trial sessions were run over the two weeks prior to the event that determined the starting positions in a 100-mile (160.9km) heat race. The finishing positions in *that* race set up the starting spots for the 500-miler. The first time trial was held on February 7, 1959, and Fireball Roberts led the pack with a speed of 140.581 mph (226.243kph).

The next day, there was no qualifying, but there was entertainment planned. Marshall Teague was set to take a run at the closed course speed record in a special Indy car. His

run that day topped out at about 172 mph (276.8kph), which was shy of the 177-mph (284.8kph) record. The team planned to make some adjustments and return for another go. They were back on track on February 11 and had cranked the speedster up to 160 mph (257.4kph) by the third lap. As Teague started into the next lap, the car lifted, slid off the track, and began to flip. Teague, and his seat, came loose from the car and landed more than 100 feet (30.4m) away from the wreckage. Marshall Teague, former AAA (American Automobile Association) racer, owner of the famous

RIGHT: *Racer Marshall Teague shares his notes with a young friend. Teague was the owner of the famous "Teague-mobile" Hudsons driven by him and Herb Thomas in the 1950s. Teague left NASCAR for the AAA ranks in 1952. The six-time Grand National winner was killed in a sports car test run at Daytona in 1959.*

Fabulous Hudson Hornet, and seven-time Grand National winner, was killed instantly.

The time trials concluded without further incident, and line-ups were set for the qualifying race. There were actually two of those—one for the Grand National division and another for NASCAR's Convertible division. To draw attention to NASCAR's Convertible division, it was decided that the first 500 would feature both hard-top and convertible cars (with hardtops lined up along the inside and ragtops on the outside), so 100-mile (160.9km) heat races were held for both groups. Shorty Rollins won the first stock car race at the track, the Convertible heat, and Bob Welborn won the correspon-ding Grand National 100 miler.

With the mixed car format, Welborn's No. 49 Chevy lined up in the pole position, with Shorty Rollins beside him in the second spot. Fritz Wilson had third and Marvin Panch's Ford convertible was fourth. When they came around for the green flag, it was imme-diately clear that the hardtops had a distinct advantage. At the speed they were running, the air turbulence around an open-roof car slowed it down, while the sleeker hardtops had less drag and could run faster. The only convertibles that seemed able to keep up were those that tucked right in behind a Grand National car and stayed in its slipstream. They didn't know it yet, but they had invented "drafting."

Bob Welborn took the green from flagman Johnny Bruner (who stood along the inside of the track to start the race) and led the first lap. Tom Pistone was also strong early on and traded the lead with Welborn through the first twenty circuits. Two Grand National drivers at the back of the pack, Fireball Roberts and Jack Smith, hooked up together (there's that drafting again) and were able to quickly move to the

front. Fireball put his Jim Stephen's Pontiac at the point for about twenty laps until his fuel pump let go and he dropped out.

As the race progressed, the high speeds and long green flag run (there were no yellow flags throughout the whole race) began to wear on the equipment, and one by one, cars fell by the wayside. By the three-quarters mark, there were only two cars left on the lead lap—and what a contrast between the drivers. One was tough old veteran Lee Petty, already a two-time champion and winner of thirty-seven races. The other was rookie Johnny Beauchamp, in only his second NASCAR race. Beauchamp was holding his own with Petty, though, in a tight battle through the closing laps. The two exchanged the lead again and again as the laps counted down. With a couple of circuits remaining, they ran up on the lapped car of Joe Weatherly. Weatherly was able to stick with the pair, and side-by-side, the three cars flew across the line for the white flag. And they stayed that way all around the track. As the competitors hurtled toward the checkered flag,

ABOVE: *Jim McGurk (No. 16) spins in the first Daytona 500 while Curtis Turner (No. 41) and Eduardo Dibos (No. 37) stamp on the brakes to avoid rear-ending Johnny Beauchamp's No. 73.*

Beauchamp enjoyed a brief moment in the sun when he was declared winner of the 1959 Daytona 500 victory— alas, the ruling didn't stand. Beauchamp did get a trophy for keeps just a month later, winning at Lakewood Speedway in Georgia.

they were still glued together, and the three cars flashed over the finish line dead even.

Who had won? The flagman and Bill France (who had been at the finish line as well) called Beauchamp the winner and the Midwesterner took his No. 73 T-Bird to victory lane. Others weren't so sure. Lee Petty was sure *he* had won. Beauchamp got to kiss the girl and hold the trophy in the winner's circle, but with all of the uncertainty, France held back the official outcome, and asked that photographers and fans who had film of the finish send it to NASCAR to review. There were lots of shots, but it took three days to find one that clearly showed the order just as they crossed the line. A reel from a *News of the Week* film showed Weatherly's car in front, but a lap down. Lee Petty's No. 42 had two feet (0.6m) on Beauchamp and was

finally declared the official winner. Charlie Griffith, in the same car Cotton Owens had won with in the 1957 beach race, came in third, and Owens himself was fourth. Joe Lee Johnson had the best finish of the Convertible drivers: sixteenth overall. The race also included a young man who would one day make his own mark on the Daytona International Speedway. Richard Petty would have to be happy with his dad's victory; the younger Petty's car had blown up after only eight laps.

The first Daytona 500 had an amazing effect on the racing world. Many motorsports pundits had predicted no race could be run on a track that large and fast without disaster. The NASCAR drivers had proven them wrong. A field of fifty-nine roared around the big track together for two hundred laps, faster than any stock car race had

ever been run, without a single incident. The race was also extremely competitive. There were thirty-three lead changes, and seven different drivers shared the lead. It was clear, though, that the equipment was not altogether up to this type of racing. More than half of the field either dropped out altogether or spent time in the pits repairing mechanical failures. Daytona would challenge the Detroit auto manufacturers to step up to the new challenges of a new era in stock car racing.

"Pipe Dream Speedway" didn't turn out to be such a stretch of the imagination after all. The race that had grown out of Bill France's vision and dedication had earned his sport a bigger, brighter future than any number of dirt track events ever could have. The Daytona 500 was a milestone and set the standard for the superspeedway era.

ABOVE: *Lee Petty and Johnny Beauchamp in the final laps of the 1959 Daytona 500. This photo was taken before the pair came up on the lapped car of Joe Weatherly, forming the famous three-way split at the finish line. One of the first "career" race car drivers in the NASCAR ranks, Petty made an effort to run in nearly all of the Grand National season events (not a common practice at the time). The points he earned in those races helped him to three NASCAR championships.*

The Superspeedway Era

The success of the Daytona 500 quickly spread. New superspeedways were built and added to the schedule throughout the 1960s, permanently changing the complexion of the sport. Many of those tracks are still in the Winston Cup schedule today: Rockingham, Atlanta, Talladega, and Michigan. The excitement of the 1959 race even convinced network TV execs to take a chance on the growing sport. CBS sent an anchorman and crew to Daytona to catch some of the 1960 Speed Weeks events. They focused on shorter races, figuring that those would have more appeal to audiences and would be easier to broadcast than the 500-miler. The ratings were high enough that NBC joined the party to broadcast a ten-lap challenge race as well.

NASCAR added a second Grand National race at Daytona late in the 1959 season. An Indy car event was planned for the Fourth of July weekend, but at the speeds those cars could run on the high banks (much faster than on any track in their normal schedule), they tended to lift off. The United States Auto Club (USAC) decided to back away until more testing could be done. France, needing to fill the bill, ran a 250-miler of his own, the Firecracker 250; Indy cars never did return to Daytona to race.

The 1960s was a period of considerable growth for the young organization, which not surprisingly experienced some growing pains. Twice in that period (1961 and 1969), drivers took steps to unionize in order to obtain concessions on purses, pensions, and safety. When Curtis Turner and Tim Flock brought in the Teamsters Union to organize drivers in 1961, Bill France threatened to "plow up my track at Daytona and plant corn in the infield." Both efforts to unionize were unsuccessful, and the first resulted in Turner and Flock being banned from NASCAR for life.

As if a premonition of the turbulence to come, the 1960 Speed Weeks were fraught with crashes and injuries. It started off with a Modified race that was stopped by a crash that collected thirty-seven cars. And it didn't end there.

The qualifying format for the 500 changed a bit that year. The front row was set by the winners of two 10-mile (16km) sprints, and the remainder of the field by finishing positions in the two 100-milers. Fireball Roberts began a tradition of dominating the qualifiers, leading the first of those from start to finish. There were two crashes in the short race. One of those, on the first lap, ended with Tommy Irwin's T-Bird half-submerged in Lake Lloyd. Irwin crashed with two other cars coming out of turn two, and his spinning car vaulted the embankment around the lake and came to rest in the water. It was possibly the only time a NASCAR race announcer got to say that a driver "swam to safety."

The racers were still learning to gauge to the effects of the air on the cars' stability at the track, and high wind speeds on the day of the 1960 Daytona 500 played havoc with the field. Multiple crashes slowed the race and a total of thirty-two laps were run under the yellow flag. Fireball Roberts led the opening laps but succumbed to a blown engine and dropped out after only fifty-one circuits. Both Lee and Richard Petty had strong entries, and they swapped the point throughout the second half of the race. As the event wound down, Florida driver Bobby Johns moved ahead of the elder Petty and started pulling away. On the backstretch, at lap 191, though, wind turbulence caused the back window to pop out of his Pontiac. The dramatic change in handling sent No. 3 spinning through the infield, stopping just short of the lake. Johns got the car started and back on track, but since there was no caution, the excursion had cost him valuable time. Junior Johnson, who had earlier moved into second place, was able to take the lead and keep it, winning by a margin of more than twenty-three seconds. The 1960 Speed Weeks did end on a positive note. John Masoni, Johnson's car owner, donated the $19,000

winning paycheck to charity. He explained that he was in the sport for fun, not profit.

Fireball Roberts once again was master of the qualifying events in 1961, winning both the pole race and his 100-mile (160.9km) qualifier (which was irrelevant since he already had the pole). He was the class of the field in the Daytona 500 as well, leading 170 of the first 187 laps. Roberts had a full lap lead on second place, his Smokey Yunick teammate, Marvin Panch, when smoke began to billow from the rear of the black and gold No. 22. Roberts coasted to the Daytona pits while Panch went on to an easy win over Joe Weatherly.

Several familiar faces were missing from the main event that year—crashes in the 100-milers had taken a high toll. There were five cautions in the first event, taking out almost a dozen cars. Near the end of the second race, Lee Petty and Johnny Beauchamp were reprising their fierce battle in the inaugural 500 when they tangled in turn three. The cars locked bumpers, turned towards the guardrail, and then both lifted up and over the railing. Rescue workers found the cars at the bottom of the embankment, and it was clear that both drivers were hurt. The injuries were serious. Though both drivers recovered, the crash effectively ended their racing careers. Petty, a three-time Grand National champion, left the sport with a record-setting (at that time) fifty-four wins.

The 1962 Speed Weeks started out with

the same old same-old—Fireball Roberts in victory lane for both the pole race and his qualifier. Roberts was one of those ace drivers, like Earnhardt and Waltrip later on, who could win just about everything at the Daytona track, except the Harley J. Earle trophy (awarded for the Daytona 500 victory and featuring a replica of Earle's Firebird 2 speedster). Roberts certainly knew his way around the Daytona track, and his cars were prepped by top mechanic (and owner of the "Best Damn Garage in Town") Smokey Yunick. While blazing fast on short runs, the cars couldn't hold together for the grueling 500 miles (804.6 km), and Roberts had yet to even finish one of the big races.

Well, 1962 was finally his year. The entire race was run without incident, and though there were five different leaders, Roberts (nicknamed "Fireball" for his blazing pitches in college baseball) had the point to himself for 144 of the 200 laps. The toughest challenge came from Richard Petty. Petty drafted behind Roberts through the second half of the event and shot around him to take the lead for a lap or two several times before Roberts reasserted himself. Fireball shook No. 43 (Petty's car) for good with about fifty laps to go and cruised to victory with twenty-seven seconds to spare. Roberts drove to the winner's circle, but the action wasn't over yet! The Petty team lodged a protest with NASCAR, complaining that Roberts had too many men "over the wall" on one of their pit stops (no more than six men at a time are allowed to service the car during stops). The matter was taken under advisement, and Roberts had to hold off the celebration for several days. Finally, NASCAR ruled in his favor, as the allegation was not substantiated in any way. Fireball Roberts had finally finished—and won—the Daytona 500.

The NASCAR All-Star Races

BILL FRANCE DID HIS BEST to pack the February Speed Weeks with racing action. In 1961, he decided to add a special invitational race that would highlight the top drivers in the sport. It was called the American Challenge Cup and was open, by invitation only, to drivers who had won major events in the previous season. Seventeen of the eighteen winners from that year were called (Glen Woods, who'd only won at the tiny Bowman-Gray track, was excluded). Eleven of those drivers accepted the invitation and formed the starting field for NASCAR's first special event.

The race was a 25-miler held the Sunday before the Daytona 500. Starting positions were determined by lottery, and Joe Weatherly got the pole. Weatherly was only concerned about leading one lap—the last one—so he dropped back a bit after the green flag. Junior Johnson took over at point, but was soon tracked down by Fireball Roberts. Roberts drew the last starting spot but charged through the small field to take over the lead.

Weatherly was playing possum to see who had the strong cars and to figure out which groove to run. He decided on the outside lane and used it on the last lap to pull up behind, then pass, Fireball. Weatherly got the win and $1,000 for his efforts.

The 1962 running lured only ten of the nineteen invited drivers, but despite a short field, it was an exciting ten laps. Weatherly and Roberts drew the exact same spots as the previous year. Roberts didn't wait but half a lap to pass the field this year, and was in the lead by the backstretch on the first lap. He stayed there for the whole event—fending off a stiff challenge from Weatherly on the last circuit. Roberts told the press that Weatherly made one small mistake that cost him the race, and that it evened them up for the 1961 finish.

The third, and final, running of the Cup was in 1963. Although all of the thirteen invited teams were at Daytona for the 500, only seven accepted the challenge. Many felt it was too much risk for too little money. Few teams had back-up cars to resort to at the time, so a crash in the invitational could take them out of the 500. Fred Lorenzen won the 1963 running, holding off fellow Holman-Moody Ford driver Nelson Stacy.

The American Challenge Cup was discontinued after 1963 due to too little interest from both fans and drivers. In the 1980s, though, the concept was revitalized and the R.J. Reynolds Tobacco Company (RJR) sponsored a "winners only" race, "The Winston." By removing the pressure of contending for championship points, "The Winston" offers drivers a chance to cut loose and just run flat-out for pride and money. With a much bigger

paycheck and incredible fan support, it's become one of the favorite events on the circuit for drivers and spectators alike.

ABOVE: *Junior Johnson led early in the first all-star race in 1961, but had to settle for third place at the stripe. Johnson's No. 27 Holly Farms Pontiac crossed the line behind Joe Weatherly and Fireball Roberts.*

LEFT: *Fireball Roberts hugs the beauty queens in Daytona's victory lane after his 1962 win in the American Challenge Cup race. Roberts and Ned Jarrett were the only two drivers to participate in all three of the all-star races.*

The 1963 Daytona 500

One of the underlying themes in stock car racing in the 1960s was the intense rivalry among the automakers and the seesaw battle of who could build the biggest, fastest engine and convince NASCAR to sanction it. And all of that was somewhat "off the record" since the companies still officially supported a ban on participation in motorsports that had been in effect since the mid-1950s.

General Motors (GM) had been the least strict about offering help to teams and as a result had ninety-seven wins to its credit, between Chevy and Pontiac, in the first three years of the decade. By 1963, Ford had had enough of the shellacking it was taking on the tracks, and more importantly, in the minds of young car buyers. The company announced that it no longer supported the ban and was into NASCAR "with both feet." First, Ford provided its sponsored teams with a new, sleek Galaxie model to race. Second, it fielded a group of talented young drivers on the main Fomoco (Ford Motor Company) factory team run by the Abbott and Costello-looking pair, John Holman and Ralph Moody. "Fast" Freddie Lorenzen, who had finished fifth in the previous Daytona 500 and hooked up with Holman-Moody, was expected to be a force. Ford also brought in some help from the USAC ranks. Dan Gurney got the first Ford win of the year on the road course at Riverside, California, and was set to run at Daytona as well.

The GM teams looked strong again in the early Speed Weeks events. Roberts put his Pontiac on the pole once more (his third straight Daytona 500 pole), and Junior Johnson, in a Ray Fox Chevy, won the first 100-mile qualifier. Another USAC entry, Johnny Rutherford, surprised the crowd by winning the second 100-miler, also in a Chevy. Ford wasn't taking any chances with

the 500, though, and accordingly stacked the deck for the Holman-Moody team with four entries for the race: Lorenzen in No. 28, Nelson Stacy in No. 29, Dan Gurney in No. 0, and Larry Frank in No. 06.

The now-fabled Wood Brothers, Glen and Leonard Wood from Virginia, ran another long-time Ford team at Daytona. Marvin Panch, an eight-time winner at that point, was their driver. Before the stock car races, though, Panch was practicing for a Speed Weeks road-course race in a Maserati sports car. The test run ended in a terrible, fiery crash. Panch was pulled from the burning wreck by several bystanders and hospitalized. Panch would rejoin the team later in the year, but the Wood Brothers were without a driver for the Daytona races.

One of the spectators who'd helped save Panch was a sometime-racer, a giant of a man everyone called "Tiny." DeWayne "Tiny" Lund had raced stock cars since 1955, but never had a steady ride and was at the beach that year to watch the races and maybe pick up a seat for one of the events. Panch asked his car owners to take a chance on the brave young man, and put him in the No. 21 Ford for the Daytona races. The team agreed and Lund went from spectator to starter.

ABOVE: *Fords line up first, second, and third in the late stages of the 1963 Daytona 500. Fred Lorenzen (No. 28) and Ned Jarrett (No. 11) were the only other cars on the lead lap with Tiny Lund at the finish.*

RIGHT: *The fourth and final pit stop for the Wood Brothers team in the 1963 500. The crew kept a careful eye on tire conditions (note the man at the right front tire), but didn't change rubber at all during the race. The team's expertise earned them a visit to Indianapolis to consult with Indy car teams on pit strategy and execution.*

The 1963 Daytona 500 was an exciting race. Eleven different drivers swapped the lead a total of thirty times in the 200 laps. The first half was all about the GM cars. Roberts led the first ten circuits, but wasn't destined to repeat his win and fell out with engine failure. Junior Johnson and G.C. Spencer in Smokey Yunick Chevys were wickedly fast, but couldn't sustain the speed and were in the garage before the halfway point.

Around that time, the Ford contingent finally began to make some noise. Larry Frank, one of the Holman-Moody drivers, led five laps but fell back and finished eleventh. Ned Jarrett, in another Ford, led three times for a total of twenty-six laps and ended up third (by virtue of which he took an early lead in the series points race). The real race for the last fifty laps, though, was between Fred Lorenzen and—you guessed it—Tiny Lund. Lorenzen's HM Ford was up front for the most laps in the race, more than seventy, and was in good position to win after everyone cycled around on their last pit stop. Lund had made a surprisingly strong run and was one of the only three cars left on the lead lap as the race wound down. When Lorenzen and then Ned Jarrett pitted for the final time, Lund was left in first. Of course, he would have to pit for gas and tires as well, cycling Lorenzen back to the leader's position—right?

Well, not exactly. Knowing that they had little chance of outmuscling the other contestants, the Wood Brothers took a different tack. First, they ran the entire race on only one set of tires. The time saved in pit stops by not changing tires—a four-tire stop at that time could take thirty seconds—kept them on the lead lap and in contention for most of the afternoon. With that advantage, they were also able to conserve fuel a bit by not having to constantly charge full-throttle to keep up, and were able to finish the race with one fewer pit stop for gas than everyone else. So after No. 28 and No. 11 pitted with about ten laps left, Lund just kept on truckin' and went on to win by twenty-four seconds over Lorenzen.

It was Lund's first Grand National win, and a storybook finish that was immensely popular with fans and fellow racers alike. It went over well with Fomoco also. They swept the top five finishing spots in the race and got the first of twenty-three wins that year. And for the Wood Brothers, it was the start of their reputation as the prima donnas of the pit stop ballet.

Motor City Madness

It was Bill France's skill at diplomacy and negotiating that proved most essential to NASCAR's continued growth over the second half of the decade, as the big boys in Detroit threw their weight around, jostling for supremacy. Back on the motorsports bandwagon, each wanted to make the most out of the exposure and image NASCAR could offer—rulebook be damned.

Chrysler countered Ford's domination of the 1963 season with a new Hemi engine designed specifically for racing, and teams lined up to join the Mopar ranks. (Mopar stands for *Motor Parts*, Chrysler's parts division, but has come to mean any car produced by Chrysler.) Despite concerns about the power plant's eligibility, NASCAR allowed it, and the Hemi made a mockery of competition in the 1964 Daytona 500. Hemis took 1-2-3 in both qualifiers. The second race was another photo finish as Richard Petty, Bobby Isaac, and Jimmy Pardue crossed the line three abreast. NASCAR wasn't worried—they had installed a special camera at the line for just this occasion—until they developed the film and

found it was blank! Once again, photos from fans and press decided a Daytona finish: Isaac by a foot (30.5cm). The actual Daytona 500 was more of the same. Petty lapped the entire field in his No. 43 Plymouth, and Pardue and Paul Goldsmith made it 1-2-3 again for Chrysler. Petty rode his Hemi to nine wins and his first Grand National championship that year.

The 1962 and 1963 Grand National champ was not in the field at Daytona that year. Joe Weatherly had been killed in a crash in the season-opening Riverside race. Weatherly never wore a shoulder harness, and there were no window nets at the time, so when his Mercury got out of shape and slapped the wall on the driver's side, his helmet hit the concrete barrier, killing him instantly.

The Hemi's total dominance in 1964 backfired on Mopar when NASCAR outlawed the engine before the 1965 season. Rather than adjust, Chrysler decided to boycott the sport and pulled its support and its team drivers. With names like Richard Petty, Bobby Isaac, and Paul Goldsmith missing from the field,

ABOVE: *Johnny Roberts catches some serious air as he flies through the infield in a 1967 Sportsmen race at Daytona. Safety window nets weren't mandatory at that point, and though the car was demolished in the terrifying accident, the driver sustained only minor injuries.*

Roberts had died from injuries sustained in a fiery crash at Charlotte Motor Speedway the previous May. Roberts won thirty-three races in only 206 starts over the course of his spectacular but too-short career.

Talk of another boycott hung over the 1966 Speed Weeks at Daytona. Ford had a new 427 overhead cam (OHC) engine that NASCAR was looking over, and threatened to pull out from competition if the power plant weren't approved. NASCAR stayed tough, and not long after Speed Weeks, Ford withdrew its support. A number of Ford and Mercury teams stuck it out through the year, long enough to notch twelve wins for the blue oval (Ford's emblem). By 1967, however, concessions were made to bring the manufacturer back into the fold. Helping Ford to make its case, Chrysler teams won both qualifiers in 1966, and Richard Petty became the first two-time winner of the Daytona 500, again lapping the entire field.

Thankfully, the focus was back on racing again for the 1967 season. Curtis Turner earned the pole position and, rather than take a chance on damaging his primo car, parked it after only one lap of his 100-mile (160.9 km) qualifying race. Series regular LeeRoy Yarbrough took the lead from USAC champ A.J. Foyt with a handful

Daytona 500 attendance dropped to half its previous 100,000 level. The race itself was a Ford romp. Fred Lorenzen won the rain-shortened event (his only Daytona 500 victory), and Fords or Mercurys took all of the top thirteen spots. It stayed that way through the first half of the season. By mid-year, NASCAR was essentially a one-marque series and was in trouble. In June, NASCAR issued new rules that compromised on the use of the Hemis, and by July, Mopar was back on track. As an added incentive to bring spectators back to the tracks, old fan-favorite Curtis Turner was reinstated (despite his failed unionizing activities in 1961).

Another superstar of NASCAR, however, was absent from the 1965 Daytona 500. Fireball

LEFT: *Marvin Panch was the Wood Brothers' driver at Daytona in 1965 and for most of the season, but the Virginia-based team also sponsored Dan Gurney (pictured here) in the Riverside race. Gurney won the event, his third straight at the California road course.*

BELOW: *Ray Fox (standing) and LeeRoy Yarbrough (in car) teamed up to run a supercharged Chrysler during Speed Weeks at Daytona in 1965. They set a new closed-course speed record of 181.818 mph (290.1kph) with the car. The engine in the car, a modified version of Mopar's Hemi, was reintroduced on the GN circuit after NASCAR finally relented from its earlier ban of the motor.*

RIGHT: *When invited to return to the NASCAR circuit in 1966, Turner ran six races with Smokey Yunick and six with the Wood Brothers. Turner drove the No. 41 for the latter organization in the Daytona 500. A broken windshield (a problem for several Fords in the field that year) sidelined him after 122 laps.*

RIGHT: *Earl Balmer (right) and Paul Goldsmith (left) share the limelight after winning one each of the Daytona qualifying races in 1966. The wins put the drivers in the second row for the start of the 500. Their smiles no doubt faded during the race, though, as Balmer's engine let go after only twenty-one laps and Goldsmith struggled to an eighteenth-place finish, making his the last car running on the track.*

of laps left in the first qualifier and used the lapped car of Tiny Lund as a "pick" to keep Foyt behind him. "Supertex," as Foyt was known, felt Lund had blocked him and threatened to pull out of the Daytona 500 if NASCAR didn't do something about it. When he was told they'd just have to "move everyone up one notch in the starting field," he changed his mind. Fred Lorenzen played it cool through the second qualifier, staying with the leaders but not battling for the lead. When Petty, Cale Yarborough (no relation to LeeRoy Yarbrough), and Mario Andretti, an Indy car driver who ran a handful of NASCAR races each season from 1966–1969, stopped for a splash-and-go of gas, Lorenzen stayed on track and took the checkered flag. He went the entire 100 miles (160.9 km) without a single pit stop.

The 1967 Daytona 500 was a battle of attrition. Twenty-eight of the fifty cars in the field spent time in the garage with mechanical failures. Curtis Turner's babied Chevy led only the opening lap before it started falling back. Approaching the halfway point, he was a lap down when his engine let go. Other front-runners Yarbrough, David Pearson, and A.J. Foyt also fell by the wayside.

The surprise factor in the race was USAC champion Andretti. The great Pennsylvania driver started in twelfth but with a potent Holman-Moody Ford was up to the front by lap twenty-three. Mario kept the blue and gold No. 11 in the front pack for the entire race as one after another of the top competitors fell off. Following a caution on lap 168, he and Fred Lorenzen were the only cars left on the lead lap. Tiny Lund (in a Petty Enterprises Plymouth) was a lap down and battled with the two leaders to try to regain his lost lap. Andretti got by, but Lund held up Lorenzen enough to let No. 11 slip away. The last several laps were run under caution (the sixth of the day), and Mario Andretti cruised under the flag stand for his only NASCAR win. The victory made him the only racer in history to win the Indy 500, NASCAR's Daytona 500, and the Formula One championship.

ABOVE: *Curtis Turner started his final Daytona 500 from the pole in Smokey Yunick's black and gold No. 13 Chevy. He led six laps in the event but dropped out early with a broken fuel pump. It was also the last race the two veterans ran as a team.*

LEFT: *Mario Andretti cruises to his first and only NASCAR victory (out of fourteen starts), in the 1967 Daytona 500. The Holman-Moody team, which also fielded the second-place finisher, was at the peak of their performance and still enjoyed strong Ford factory sponsorship.*

Chapter Two

AERO WARRIORS

AS WE'VE SEEN, NASCAR'S FIRST TWO DECADES were dominated by its relationship with the Detroit auto manufacturers. It was a love-hate affair that helped make stock car racing successful but also kept it hanging on the brink of disaster.

Bill France knew that the automakers were the ones who made it possible for many teams to get the parts and assistance they needed to be competitive, so he welcomed their involvement. As long as there were several different car makes in close competition, the racing was exciting and the sport would grow. The auto companies weren't particularly interested in close racing though—they wanted to see their brand sitting in victory lane after every race. "Win on Sunday, sell on Monday" was a fact of life and fueled the companies' interest, so NASCAR's early history was a succession of balancing acts—concessions to one and then another manufacturer to keep their cars on the track and their dollars flowing to teams.

As though that weren't tough enough, from the mid-1950s to the mid-1960s that manufacturer involvement was reluctant and more or less undercover. In 1955, a terrible crash in the 24 Hours of Le Mans race left more than one hundred spectators dead when a car careened off course and into a crowd. The backlash against all forms of motorsports was severe. In the aftermath of the Le Mans disaster, and mindful of the ever-increasing

ABOVE: *Richard Petty drove only one season of his thirty-five year career in a Ford—1969. The Ford setup was pretty good, and the team won ten races and finished second in points. It wasn't good enough to overcome the Petty's longtime allegiance to Chrysler, though—the next season Richard was back in a Plymouth.*

LEFT: *Cale Yarborough receives the top-of-the-line pit service from the Wood Brothers crew at the 1968 Daytona 500. A testament to just how good the Wood Brothers were, Yarborough set the track speed record during the trials and then went on to win the 500 in dominant fashion, coming from far back to catch leader LeeRoy Yarbrough in the final five laps of the race.*

number of deaths from crashes on U.S. highways, the Automobile Manufacturers Association issued to its members a ban on participation in all forms of motorsports.

Ford, General Motors, and Chrysler were the auto manufacturers running in NASCAR at the time, and all three complied with the ban—outwardly at least. Semon "Bunkie" Knudsen, CEO at General Motors, realized that there was substantial value to his cars outperforming the competition on the stock car tracks and unofficially allowed parts and assistance to go to Pontiac, Chevy, and Oldsmobile teams. With the smash success of the 1959 Daytona 500, the other manufacturers quickly became wise to the potential as well, and the dam began to leak.

NASCAR knew it couldn't live without the automakers, but once they were back in full force, NASCAR also learned how difficult it would be to live with them. The original principles of "strictly stock" had long ago gone by the boards. In 1966, Junior Johnson responded to a NASCAR ruling that his car wasn't "production" with the argument, "There isn't anything production about a stock car. A production car wouldn't last three laps at Daytona and there's never been a production engine raced in NASCAR with any success. Who does France think he's kidding?" The ruling principle throughout the 1960s was, instead, parity. As each manufacturer came out with a new and improved engine or car model, NASCAR battled to avoid having that model take over the series. When they tried outlawing a component, the factories conveniently fell back to the still-in-force motorsports ban and pulled their support: Chevy in 1963, Chrysler in 1965, and Ford in 1966—one boycott after another kept Bill France's rulebook in a steady state of flux for the whole decade.

Fastbacks and Wings

As the manufacturers sank money into stock car racing, the performance of the models steadily improved. Early modifications focused on engine size and power. As drivers and engineers began to better understand the effects of aerodynamics on speed, and as more and more large tracks were built where aero-dynamics were a factor, greater focus was placed on the shape of the race cars.

Mopar teams had ruled the roost in stock car racing through 1966 and 1967, winning seventy of the ninety-eight races in those years. That was due in large part to Richard Petty's incredible and unparalleled string of twenty-seven victories in 1967 (and his second championship), but the team of up-and-comer David Pearson and veteran car builder Cotton Owen made an impression as well in their slick-backed Dodge Charger. The Charger was the first of the fastbacks to hit the circuit. It was radical for the time, but turned out to be just the first shot fired in what would become the "aero wars."

Two years of Chrysler domination was more than enough for Ford, and in 1968, they retaliated with two new models, the Mercury Cyclone and Ford Torino. They were long, low fastbacks that sliced through the air and had sloped rear windows for improved rear down-force and stability. Daytona speeds went up dramatically. The 1967 pole winner, Curtis Turner, ran 180.831 mph (291.019kph). Cale Yarborough put the Woods Brothers Cyclone on the 1968 pole at 189.222 mph (304.523kph), almost a nine-mph (14.48kph) jump. Dodge had a new model as well, the Charger 500, but it wasn't a match, and the balance swung back to the "blue oval gang."

More of the same occurred in 1969— at least at first. Ford upped the ante with improved versions of their hot rods, the Cyclone Spoiler II and the Torino Talladega. The latter was named after the latest NASCAR speed palace, Talladega Super-speedway in Alabama. That track set the new standard for record-setting runs and, with higher banking and broader turns, supported speeds even higher than those achieved at Daytona.

LEFT: *Two of the greatest American auto racers, A.J. Foyt (left) and Mario Andretti (right), both tried their hands at NASCAR racing. The two open-wheel racers are shown here before the 1968 Firecracker 400. It was one of Andretti's last stock car runs, but Foyt contin-ued running Winston Cup events well into the 1990s.*

Chrysler wasn't ready to throw in the towel, though. Dodge engineers had been working on a new model, based on the Charger, that looked like it would blow away all of the competition. When Richard Petty was given a preview of the car, he immediately asked when he could take one to the track. In a monumental blunder of bureaucracy, Dodge officials told their superstar that he was on the Plymouth team and, therefore, not eligible for the new Dodge. Faced with a repeat of his less-than stellar 1968 season, Petty did the unthinkable and switched to Ford for 1969.

The Dodge Daytona debuted at Talladega for the inaugural race in September 1969. The car was unlike any other. Instead of the usual flat front grille of that day, it had an aerodynamic, bullet nose that reduced drag (and thus increased speed) tremendously. At the other end, a huge wing rose over the back deck for increased stability at the high speeds it could reach. The pole speed for the Talladega race was set by the new "wing car" at 196.286 mph (315.891kph), and the fastest qualifying speed (in second-day trials for the back half of the field) was more than 199 mph (320.2kph). Dodge was back in business and picked up seven wins in the last eleven races. For 1970, Chrysler released a Plymouth version of the car, the Superbird (based on the Plymouth Roadrunner), and lured Petty Enterprises back to Dodge. Chrysler was back on top of the aero war, and Dodge/Plymouth teams set speed records. With Buddy Baker the first driver to break the 200-mph barrier, running 200.447 mph (322.588kph) in a test session at Talladega, Dodge/Plymouth dominated the superspeedway events through the year.

Where was General Motors through all of this? The company essentially sat out the whole aero car episode. GM had backed away from racing support in the mid-1960s and wasn't a real force again until a decade later.

The 1968 Daytona 500

The Ford teams were loaded for bear for the tenth annual running of the Great American Race. Gone were the Galaxies, replaced by Ford Torinos and Mercury Cyclones—cars that just plain *looked* fast.

BELOW: *David Pearson collects his thoughts during a championship 1968 season. The combination of Pearson's driving talent and Holman-Moody's mechanical wizardry made the No. 17 Ford team nearly unbeatable in 1968 and '69.*

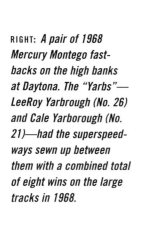

RIGHT: *A pair of 1968 Mercury Montego fast-backs on the high banks at Daytona. The "Yarbs"—LeeRoy Yarbrough (No. 26) and Cale Yarborough (No. 21)—had the superspeedways sewn up between them with a combined total of eight wins on the large tracks in 1968.*

Cale Yarborough, in the Wood Brothers No. 21, LeeRoy Yarbrough in Junior Johnson's No. 26, and David Pearson in the Holman-Moody No. 17 were among the top Ford teams itching to run their hot new cars. Mario Andretti and Donnie Allison also fielded Holman-Moody entries. Richard Petty had a new model Plymouth Roadrunner, replacing the unbeatable Belvedere of the year before. The car had an interesting cosmetic feature—a black vinyl roof. Rumor in the garage had it that the rough texture of the vinyl helped to break up airflow and make the car faster. Others thought it was hiding some illegal change the team had made to the roof. The Petty team smiled mischievously but offered no comment.

One other team that was definitely up to mischief was Smokey Yunick's. Yunick brought a Chevy Chevelle to the track that he thought could compete with the fast Fords and Chryslers. He had good reason to believe that, and the NASCAR inspectors, suspecting rule infractions, tore the car down, coming up with a list of nine illegal modifications that had to be corrected before it would be allowed to qualify. Racing lore has it that Yunick looked at the list, shook his head and tersely commented, "Better make it ten," before getting in the car and driving it away. The inspectors were scratching their heads over his comment until they noticed that the car's gas tank had been removed and was still lying there on the ground. Neither the overpumped Chevy nor its listed driver, Gordon Johncock, made it onto the track.

The time trials for the front row and the 125-mile (201.1km) qualifier-race lineups (up from 100 miles [160.9km] in previous years) showed just how quick the new Fords were. Fomoco logged seven of the eight fastest times, and the polesitter, Cale Yarborough, ran a lap at 189.222 mph (304.523kph), by far the fastest NASCAR speed up to that time. Richard Petty put his Plymouth on the outside of the front row.

Heavy rains soaked the track on the day of the 125-mile qualifying races. During a brief respite in the downpour, Bill France tried to get the races in, although all but one driver (rookie Dave Marcis) felt the track was too wet and refused to run. France threatened to suit up himself and run the race with just him and Marcis "if the hot shots don't want to run." He had driven his family car into the garage to do just that before the rains started again and settled the argument. The races were canceled.

The field lined up on Sunday based on the time trial speeds. Yarborough and Petty were on the front row, with LeeRoy Yarbrough and David Pearson behind them. USAC was again well represented. A.J. Foyt and Mario Andretti were joined by Al Unser in his first Daytona race.

The 500 turned into a battle of the "Yarbs." Battle was an accurate description—there were a record eleven yellow flags with sixty laps run under caution, almost a third of the event. Cale Yarborough took off from the pole to lead the first twelve circuits, then ran into trouble when his engine began to misfire. The Wood Brothers solved the problem and got him back on track, but just a few laps later he was back on pit road with ignition trouble—the engine was cutting out. Once again, they were up to the task, but the pole sitter ended up a lap down to the leaders in the aftermath.

David Pearson, Richard Petty, and Al Unser took brief turns at the point until LeeRoy Yarbrough worked his way up front

at lap twenty-eight. Yarbrough swapped the position with Mario Andretti's No. 11 through the first half of the race. Buddy Baker (son of two-time Grand National champ Buck Baker) looked strong in a Ray Fox Dodge. A member of the "Alabama Gang" (a group of drivers based in that region), Bobby Allison, had a solid run as well. Allison was driving for car owner Bondy Long, who had won the 1965 NASCAR championship with Ned Jarrett as his wheelman. Ford had moved Allison from the Holman-Moody team to make room for David Pearson, promising Allison a chance to run every race with Long and go for the championship if he performed well. Before the year was half over, though, Ford backed off that commitment and started cutting the team's schedule, despite Allison's second-place point standing. Bobby quit to pursue a full-time ride elsewhere.

The numerous cautions were a godsend to Cale Yarborough. His car, despite the early mishaps, was "running like Jack the Bear," and he was able to get his lost lap back on one of the yellow flags. By lap eighty-nine, he had worked his way back to the lead. The second half of the competition was all about Yarborough and Yarbrough.

It looked like Cale's luck changed with the eleventh caution, though, and he found himself mired in lapped traffic on the restart. LeeRoy got free quickly and sped off to a sizeable lead. Once Yarborough's No. 21 cleared the slower cars, it was evident who was the class of the field. Lap by lap, Cale narrowed the lead until, with five laps to go, he'd closed up on No. 26's rear bumper. He cleared the last obstacle and made the pass for the lead on lap 197, then set sail. Although LeeRoy had led the most laps, he had to settle for second place while Yarborough earned his fourth NASCAR win (and the first of six that year). Bobby Allison took third for a 1-2-3 sweep for Ford, and Al Unser gave Dodge its sole top-five spot by finishing in fourth place.

BELOW: *The LeeRoy Yarbrough/Junior Johnson No. 98 team was the first to win the Grand National "trifecta" of the Daytona 500, World 600, and Southern 500. In later days the feat would have earned Yarbrough the Winston Million; in 1969, it earned him the Driver of the Year award.*

Upping the Stakes: 1969–1971

Although the aero wars really heated up in 1969 and 1970, the Daytona races in those years were less about the make of the car than about pit and tire strategy.

The field looked pretty even for the 1969 Speed Weeks. Ford strutted its stuff in the first qualifier with David Pearson breaking the 190-mph (305.7kph) mark for the first time and leading a top-five sweep for that manufacturer. Dodge's teams ran much the same in the second race, with Bobby Isaac taking the checkered flag in No. 71, ahead of Charlie Glotzbach and Paul Goldsmith. Buddy Baker had won the pole in Ray Fox's No. 3 Dodge but opted to sit out the

qualifier a la Curtis Turner in 1967. And where was Richard Petty? The Petty team had switched to the fast Fords that year but hadn't quite worked out the change yet. Despite a victory in the previous race at Riverside, they were not competitive at the big track.

That year's 500 was plagued by wrecks, though they were mostly due to tire problems. At that time, teams had a choice of two types

Immediate return on investment: young Pete Hamilton had just been named to a second Petty Enterprises Superbird in 1970 when he nailed the big one, the Daytona 500. The Massachusetts driver's promising career was cut short (to just six seasons) due to a recurring neck injury.

limits, and sixteen of the entrants fell off during the race.

The surprise performer was a blond youngster from Massachusetts, Pete Hamilton. Hamilton, despite having only run parts of two previous seasons, had been tapped by Petty to drive his second car, the No. 40 Superbird. The rookie who had sneaked up to the front to lead for a couple of laps and managed to remain one of the few cars left on the lead lap as the race wore down, didn't look strong enough to challenge the 1969 Grand National champ, David Pearson, for the win. As the teams made pit stops during the final caution of the day, at lap 187, Pearson took just two new right side tires. Hamilton's team changed all four tires on his car. It's almost always the case that four fresh tires beat two, and it certainly made the difference that day. Hamilton slid past Pearson on the restart and pulled away. Pearson fought hard to keep up with the blue winged car, but couldn't get the bite he needed with two older tires and had to settle for second. Pete Hamilton celebrated his first NASCAR victory in the best way possible—in Daytona's winner's circle!

The 1970 Speed Weeks events were run under a black cloud, following the death of driver Talmidge "Tab" Prince in the second qualifying race. Participating in his very first NASCAR race, Prince was hit broadside by another driver and killed by the impact. Prince was the sixteenth NASCAR racer to be killed in a racing accident.

Hamilton visited the Daytona victory lane again the next year after the first of the 125-mile (201.1km) qualifying races. Chrysler teams were back to running Dodge Chargers and a new model Plymouth Satellite in place of the winged cars, but remained competitive. Hamilton had lost his Petty ride when Chrysler consolidated its support and replaced him with the higher-profile Buddy Baker. A.J. Foyt, now in the Woods Brothers' Mercury, had the race in hand but had to slow a bit on the last lap to avoid a spinning car. It was just enough to let Hamilton pull up to him, and the cars

of tires to run: soft compound (which was less durable but gave a better grip on the track) and hard compound (which was more durable but didn't handle as well). Blown tires, as teams pushed the edge on the better-handling soft tires, took out previous year's winner Yarborough, Paul Goldsmith, and others.

When the leaders made their last pit stops, Cotton Owens put hard compound rubber on his No. 6 Dodge, driven by Charlie Glotzbach. Junior Johnson, owner of LeeRoy Yarbrough's No. 26, had nothing to lose and rolled the dice with the soft tires. The tires held together, and the handling advantage let Yarbrough catch and pass Glotzbach for the trophy.

It was the same in 1970. Despite the appearance of the magnificent Dodge Daytonas and Plymouth Superbirds (and the fact that Richard Petty was back in one of them), the battle was determined more by pit calls than by car model. Both camps suffered a high degree of mechanical failure in the 1970 Daytona 500 as they ran at their performance crossed the line side-by-side. Hamilton's No. 6 Plymouth had the edge by just a couple of feet.

A.J. Foyt was strong in the 500 as well, and led six times (one of eleven drivers to do so) for more than forty laps. The Texan had the point and a decent lead with thirty-nine laps to go, but the normally infallible Wood Brothers had cut the fuel window too close, and No. 21 ran out of gas on the backstretch. By the time he'd coasted around to the pits and refueled, he was a lap down. Richard Petty and his teammate, Buddy Baker (in the Day-Glo red No. 11 Charger), finished first and second, respectively. It was Petty's third Daytona 500 win and the fifth for Petty Enterprises.

Back to Basics

With the back-and-forth one-upsmanship of the aero wars, NASCAR had a new concern to deal with as it faced the 1970s. The speeds reached by the Talladegas, Daytonas, and Superbirds put drivers at the ragged edge of disaster, and folks were getting pretty nervous about it.

In response, changes were made in the 1971 NASCAR rulebook specifically to reduce the speeds of the fastest car models. Winged cars were targeted with engine size limitations that essentially made them obsolete. Carburetor restrictor plates, which restrict the flow of air to the engine and cut horsepower, were also used to trim speeds at the biggest tracks.

The moves certainly had an effect. The 1971 Daytona pole speed was down 12 mph (19.3kph) from the previous year. The aero wars were over, although the knowledge gained through those years became fundamental to stock car racing success and has been applied to the design and building of race cars ever since.

And All Fall Down

Strangely, the auto manufacturers didn't put up as big a fuss as expected over the new rules. It soon became apparent why. Before everyone could catch their breath for the next go-round, the bottom dropped clean out from under the sport. Chrysler announced at the end of the 1970 season that it was drastically cutting back its support of race teams. The only team they backed in 1971 was Petty Enterprises. Dodge and Plymouth teams, including car owner Nord Krauskopf's 1970 championship team with Bobby Isaac at the wheel, went from the penthouse to the outhouse. As NASCAR reeled on the ropes from that decision, Ford delivered the knockout blow. Shortly before the 1971 season started, the company pulled completely out of stock car racing.

For twenty years, NASCAR teams had relied on auto manufacturers to supply parts and continuously redesign their cars for a competitive edge. By 1971, that was all gone and NASCAR was, perhaps, at its lowest point. "Big Bill" France was a fighter, though, and had always managed to stay one step ahead of disaster. Even as the factories were waving goodbye, France was making a deal that would not only keep the sport alive but also propel it to unexpected heights over the next thirty years.

BELOW: *Buck Baker (left) and Tiny Lund (right) talk shop at Daytona in 1971. Baker made a strong showing at the 500 that year, coming in second place, just behind Petty Enterprises teammate Richard Petty.*

Chapter Three

THE MODERN ERA

THE LOVE OF RACING IS WHAT BRINGS the drivers, car owners, and mechanics to the sport, but it's a fact of life that sponsorship dollars are what lets them continue to build competitive cars and take them to a track to race.

At the very beginning of NASCAR, the cars really were strictly stock, so the costs of running a team were manageable for any-one who had a family car to drive to the track. Over the years, as modifications and improvements were allowed, competitive race cars had to be designed and built. The teams with access to the latest parts and best shop equipment had a distinct advantage. That access cost serious money, so the teams with sponsor-ship—and before 1972 that meant being a factory team—were the winners week in and week out. The have-nots, or so-called "independents," soldiered along working with limited support, often from other race teams, and what winnings they could manage with a low-budget entry. The big names got the lion's share of trophies and attention, but they were few in number, so without the "indies," there wouldn't be any races.

ABOVE: *Race fans had a close-up view of 1983 Daytona 500 winner Cale Yarborough at work in 1983. CBS' first live-feed, in-car camera can be seen on the left side of this photo. The in-car camera has proven vastly popular over the years, giving fans an accurate idea of what the driver sees as he whips around the track. Technology has progressed quite a bit since then, of course: the same setup today is only the size of a deck of playing cards.*

LEFT: *A restart in the 1973 Daytona 500. The cars then didn't have the multitude of sponsor decals that they do today, but their paint schemes were every bit as brightly and variously colored.*

At the end of 1970, the playing field was leveled. The factories pulled out and, with really only one exception, *no one* had significant sponsorship. NASCAR saw that the situation could develop in several ways, and none of them would be good for the sport. As exciting as Richard Petty's 1967 streak of twenty-seven wins was, having one driver continuously dominate the series would only lead to disaster. With no sponsor money, the general level of competition and quality of racing would suffer and the sport would stagnate.

Junior Saves the Day

Driver-turned-car-owner Junior Johnson didn't have much schooling, but he had more common sense than most and saw the writing on the wall as the 1970 season wound down. The only way to keep his team intact was to find a top quality sponsor. Through an acquaintance in the company, Junior contacted the headquarters of the R.J. Reynolds Tobacco Company (RJR). It turned out to be the move that saved NASCAR racing.

The executives at RJR were very interested in Junior's proposal. In fact they were so enthusiastic that Johnson saw a bigger opportunity than just having them put their brand name on the quarter-panel of his car. In the late 1960s, the health hazards of cigarette use became public knowledge, and the type and extent of advertising available to tobacco companies had been severely limited by law. When the folks at RJR saw the size of the crowd at Daytona, the potential for reaching a mass audience through racing was clear. Johnson selflessly proposed that RJR talk with Bill France about sponsoring not his team but the entire series.

The deal came together quickly. Starting with the 1971 season, Reynolds would directly sponsor a race at Talladega (the Winston 500) and a championship points fund of $100,000. The company wanted to focus on the biggest events, so only races of 250 miles (402.3km) or more were covered in this sub-series called the Winston Cup. In 1972, there were almost fifty Grand National races, all of which counted for the championship trophy, but only the Winston Cup finishes were counted toward the RJR fund.

Reynolds' involvement gave the series the lift it needed to get past the auto manufacturers' exodus. It infused money into the series but more importantly attracted the attention of other big companies, which would shortly follow RJR's lead and bring much-needed support to the race teams. For their part, Reynolds opened up an entire new venue for advertising its products—one that wasn't yet regulated. It was a win-win situation, and the partnership has prospered and remains intact more than thirty years later.

Farewell to Old Friends

The institution of the Winston Cup certainly didn't solve all of the problems facing NASCAR overnight. But it did get the series moving in the right direction. Another change was planned for the 1972 season, a drastic one, to help curb teams' costs and to modernize the sport's image a bit.

In 1971, the Grand National boys ran forty-eight races and twenty-two of them were on short tracks of a half a mile (.8km) or less. The track at Islip Speedway in New York was only one fifth of a mile (.32km) long, and the race only 46 miles (74km) long. The thirty-three cars crammed onto that fifth of a mile averaged less than 50 mph (80.4kph) through the brief run. Events like that were part of NASCAR's history but didn't help to convey the sense of Grand National racing as a premier series. Further, they were too small and local to be of any interest to RJR, the series sponsor.

J.D. McDuffie set a record for futility, never winning once in 653 starts over twenty-nine years, but he proved that will power alone could overcome lack of a corporate sponsor (a luxury he never enjoyed). While RJR was taking over responsibility for the entire NASCAR schedule, McDuffie soldiered on alone. Tragically, he died during a race in 1991 when the suspension on his car failed, sending him into the wall at Watkins Glen at nearly 170 mph (273kph).

In 1972, the Grand National series was cut down from forty-eight to thirty-one races. All remaining events were on half-mile (.8km) or larger tracks and were more than 250 miles (402.3km) in length. All were run on paved tracks; the last dirt track race in the series schedule (won by Richard Petty) was run in September 1970 at the State Fairgrounds Speedway in Raleigh, North Carolina. R.J. Reynolds then sponsored the entire series, and all races counted toward the points fund. It was to be known as the Grand National Winston Cup. Historically, it is considered the start of the "modern era" of stock car racing.

The reduction cut down the travel costs for teams, but gone were many of the tracks that had been part of NASCAR's earliest days. Hickory, Nashville, and Columbia Speedways were no longer used; neither was the treacherous dirt track at Asheville-Weaverville; and Greenville Pickens and Smokey Mountain

speedways were among the casualties as well. Many of the facilities continued to operate, hosting Sportsman races (NASCAR's minor league that would develop into the Busch Grand National series), but they wouldn't share in the growing fortunes of the Winston Cup. Only the Martinsville and North Wilkesboro tracks remained on the schedule from NASCAR's first season in 1949. Martinsville is still going strong, with two races on the Winston Cup circuit today.

The Torch Is Passed

There were a few more changes of note prior to the start of the 1972 season. One of the biggest stories of the year was the retirement of NASCAR founder "Big Bill" France. The sixty-two-year-old France handed the reins of the racing series over to his oldest son, Bill Jr.

The scramble for corporate sponsorship set the stage for changes among several of the

big-name teams. The championship-winning Holman-Moody team closed its doors after the 1971 season. The operation had long been a Ford factory team, and the loss of that base was more than they could compensate for. That cut loose their 1971 driver, Bobby Allison, who, with sponsorship dollars from Coca-Cola, went shopping for a new ride. Junior Johnson, without the RJR backing he'd sought, nearly closed down his shop. He was able to keep the team going with financial help from furniture magnate Richard Howard, but couldn't resist the sponsor money tied to Bobby Allison. So Junior's 1971 driver, Charlie Glotzbach, was out and Allison and Coca-Cola were in.

Richard Petty was still the biggest name in stock car racing and was able to supplement the limited Chrysler funding he received with money from what would become the longest-lasting team sponsor relationship in the sport. STP, which stands for Studebaker Treatment of Petroleum, added their bright red logo to the Petty blue No. 43 Plymouth in 1972.

With the changes in the series schedule in 1972, the twin 125-mile (201.1km) qualifiers were no longer points races. The events were still run but solely to determine the starting field for the 500. The first of those races that year was interrupted by a thirteen-car crash that ended with the death of veteran driver Raymond "Friday" Hassler.

The 1972 Daytona 500 was not the most exciting running of the February race. Pole sitter Bobby Isaac lost the engine of his K&K Insurance Dodge after only nineteen laps. Richard Petty gave the best performance, putting on a charge to the front from thirty-second place in only twenty laps. Petty dueled with A.J. Foyt over the next sixty laps but then lost a valve in his engine and headed for the garage. From then on, it was all Foyt. A.J. led all of the remaining circuits and finished the race alone in the lead lap.

It was the Texan's first Daytona 500 win and an impressive addition to his racing resume.

Once he had the Daytona trophy, Foyt decided to focus more on USAC racing and departed the top-drawer Wood Brothers ride. He was back for the 1973 Daytona and a couple of other races that year, but in his own No. 50 car. In his place in No. 21 was David Pearson. Pearson and the Wood Brothers were a match made in racing heaven. Engine problems took them out of the 1972 Daytona, but they won just about everything else they ran that year, and for many years to come.

Coo Coo Marlin (father of current Winston Cup driver Sterling Marlin) was the surprise winner in the first qualifier in 1973. Buddy Baker, new to the No. 71 car (rumor was that he quit Petty Enterprises after the 1972 season because he was expected to stay *behind* King Richard), took the pole and the other qualifier.

As the Sunday race wore down it looked like Buddy would finally get the 500 win. He led most of the race, 157 of 200 laps, but on the last round of pit stops, Petty went with a quicker "gas only" stop and came back out on the track ahead of Baker. The "Gentle Giant," as the sometimes-tempestuous Baker was affectionately known, had the better car and was hungry for the win. Lap by lap, he closed in on Petty until, with only a handful of circuits left, his motor went up in a cloud of smoke. Petty went on to win with a two-lap margin over Bobby Isaac.

ABOVE: *Richard Petty (No. 43) passes the lapped car of Ed Negre on the way to winning the 1973 Daytona 500. Negre was a longtime Grand National racer. He hung up his helmet in 1979, having run cars for himself and other drivers (including Dale Earnhardt) since 1955 without a win.*

The Long Arm of OPEC

There was no Daytona 500 in 1974. Instead the organizers ran the Daytona 450. Due to American participation in the Arab-Israeli war in 1973, there was an oil embargo against the United States that caused widespread gasoline shortages. NASCAR willingly cooperated with government fuel conservation efforts. The voluntary move also helped avert a government crackdown on motorsports. The race, along with the ancillary Speed Weeks events, was cut by 10 percent and officially started on lap twenty-one.

The 1974 event was action-packed. There were ten cautions and an amazing fifty-seven lead changes among fourteen different drivers. It came down to Petty and Donnie Allison (younger brother of Bobby Allison), in his new DiGard ride owned by Mike DiProspero and Bill and Jim Gardner. Allison had a car length on No. 43 with ten laps to go when he cut down a tire on debris and fell off the pace. Petty went on to his fifth Daytona 500 win ahead of Yarborough, Ramo Stott, and Coo Coo Marlin. Marlin had been running in second, but miscalculated his laps and took his foot off the gas at the white flag instead of the checkered.

David Pearson's Woods Brothers' Mercury had blown up in the first two Daytonas he ran with it, but it held up all the way in 1975. The "Fox" (and later the "Silver Fox," as he was known for his calculated approach to races) had a comfortable lead on Benny Parsons with just a few laps to go. Then Richard Petty, who was laps down due to tire problems, hooked up in a draft with Parsons and helped him close in on No. 21. Pearson stomped on it, but in the rush to keep his lead, tangled with another car and went spinning. Parsons, the 1973 Winston Cup

BELOW: *The start of the 1974 Daytona "450." The race was listed as 200 laps, but the first twenty were scratched to conserve fuel (as a nod to the OPEC oil crisis). Many NASCAR races have been cut short at the back end due to track or weather conditions, but this was the only one to drop laps from the start. If the race had been another twelve laps shorter, there would have been a different winner, Donnie Allison, who blew a tire while leading with only a dozen to go.*

LEFT: *The DiGard team featuring driver Donnie Allison sported a new paint job for the 1975 season and got to show it off on the pole of the Daytona 500. Alas, fuel pump problems dropped them to a twenty-eighth-place finish, right behind the other DiGard team entry, with Johnny Rutherford.*

champ, called the unexpected win "the biggest day of my life" and thanked Petty for the assistance. David Pearson was just as outspoken about the finish, though not in a happy way, and accused Petty of playing favorites in helping Parsons. The fierce battles between Petty and Parsons would become a familiar feature of NASCAR competition for many years and would bring the sport some of its most memorable moments.

The 1976 Daytona 500

R.J. Reynolds' funding of the Winston Cup laid the foundation NASCAR needed for the future. On top of that, the infusion of corporate sponsorship dollars to more and more teams through the second half of the 1970s (and beyond) helped keep the sport moving forward. And fueling that investment more than anything was the broadcasting of NASCAR races on network television.

ABC Sports had actually contracted with NASCAR as far back as 1969, and by 1975,

CBS and ABC were showing highlights and even tape-delayed broadcasts of several races. The ratings had always been good, so for the 1976 Daytona 500, ABC made a significant commitment—to broadcast the end of the race live. It turned out to be an inspired move.

That year's Speed Weeks started out on a sour note. The time trials for the main race showed a wide discrepancy among the speeds of the cars. Stout cars like Petty's, Baker's, and Yarborough's were running in the 178–179-mph (286.4–288kph) range, while a couple of teams, A.J. Foyt's and Hoss Ellington's No. 28, Dave Marcis's No. 71, and Darrell Waltrip's DiGard No. 88, were running at 186 mph (299.3kph) or better. Although the cars had been inspected right before qualifying, the NASCAR inspectors decided to take another look at them. After a while, they announced that Foyt's and Waltrip's times were disallowed due to suspicious extra fuel lines on the cars, which were likely hooked to nitrous oxide bottles. Nitrous (a.k.a. laughing gas) gives an engine an added boost of horse-

power and was a common cheat used through the years to get an extra fast lap. Marcis' time was also disallowed due to a deviation in the front air dam.

It turned out later that many of the slower qualifiers could actually run quite a bit quicker. One driver let it slip that many of the teams had gotten together in the garage over their suspicions and decided to make sure that the target teams stood out to inspectors by deliberately running slower than them. It worked, though NASCAR wasn't happy with the attention the affair got—especially when Marcis and Waltrip came back to win the qualifying races.

All of the upset resulted in one of most unexpected starting front rows in Daytona history. USAC driver and a sometime NASCAR racer since 1969, Ramo Stott, had the pole. Raw rookie Terry Ryan in his very first NASCAR race flanked Stott. The penalized Waltrip and Marcis started in the second row (thanks to their qualifier wins), Buddy Baker had the fifth spot, followed by Richard Petty and David Pearson.

Terry Ryan did actually get to lead a lap in the race, but not until the twelfth time around. Buddy Baker leapt out from fifth place to lead the opening laps. The man on the move right from the start, though, was A.J. Foyt. Clearly ticked off about his penalty, he tore through the field with a vengeance, starting from the thirty-first spot to which he had been relegated. By lap forty, he was at the front and dueled with Petty, Pearson, and the previous year's winner, Benny Parsons. It wouldn't last, though—his engine let go on lap 143 and he coasted to the garage.

Engine failures ran rampant that day, dropping many of the top teams out of the race. Yarborough, Waltrip, Baker, and Allison all ended up behind pit wall. The battle through the last sixty laps was to be decided among No. 21, No. 43, and Parson's No. 72. With twenty-five laps left, Parsons fell off the pace; his Chevy had dropped a cylinder. Petty and Pearson stayed together, with Petty sliding by to take the lead as they raced under the white flag.

Pearson had a reputation for not showing his full strength until the right moment came.

RIGHT: *It may not be pretty, but it was a winner! David Pearson crouches next to the crushed front-end of his just-barely-drivable Purolator Mercury after winning the 1976 Daytona 500. Even years later Pearson and Petty disagree over who was to blame for the famous wreck at the end of the race.*

BELOW: *The dramatic finish of the 1976 500. Petty's car sits helpless, not far from the start/finish line (just below the flag stand, visible at the bottom of the photo). Pearson and Joe Frasson appear to be stopped farther up the track, at the start of the tri-oval. Soon after, Pearson nursed his damaged car through the grass toward the finish line and captured the win.*

Going into the third turn on the last lap was that moment. Pearson used the draft to sling-shot under Petty. The five-time winner of the Great American Race wasn't finished, though, and came right back in the fourth turn. As they sped onto the front straightaway, they were door-to-door. Heading into the tri-oval, the cars touched. The contact was enough to send Pearson headfirst into the wall, his car brushing Petty's rear quarter-panel as he turned. Petty hung on for a second, and then went spinning as well. Pearson slid down into the pit road entrance where he collected Joe Frasson's No. 18 car. Petty slapped the wall farther on, then slid into the infield of the tri-oval, coming to a stop about one hundred feet (30.5m) shy of the start/finish line. The third-place car was a full lap down and was no threat to catch up, so all Petty needed to do was limp that short distance to manage the win. His STP Dodge had stalled in the grass when he stopped, though, and Petty couldn't get it to refire. Pearson had mashed his clutch as he went around and kept his Mercury running. The Purolator car was battered, but he got it moving and nursed it through the grass, past Petty, and across the line for his first Daytona 500 victory.

The Yarborough Years

Here's a trivia question for you: Which driver was the first to run in a Grand National or Winston Cup race, Richard Petty, David Pearson, Cale Yarborough or Bobby Allison? Most folks would probably choose Petty—after all, he'd started all the way back in 1958—but the correct answer is Yarborough. The tough little South Carolinian ran his first Grand National race in 1957, and he got better and better over the next couple of decades.

Yarborough had several top rides through the 1960s—Banjo Matthews' No. 27 Ford and the Wood Brothers' No. 21—but split from NASCAR when the factory pullout occurred. He spent most of 1971 and 1972 trying his hand at USAC racing. That venture didn't pan out, so Cale was back at the stock car tracks looking for a full-time ride for the 1973 season. Bobby Allison and Junior Johnson had not hit it off all that well (although they had a decent record), so Allison left that team after the 1972 season. Yarborough took over the seat in Johnson's car, the No. 11 Chevy. The team clicked, amassing seventeen wins in its first three seasons, with two second-place finishes in the championship points. Then, in 1976, the Johnson team turned up the heat. Nine wins and the first Winston Cup championship for both driver and owner followed.

The team was strong again at the start of 1977, and Yarborough blew by the competition to win one of the Daytona qualifying races (Petty won the other). Scoring for the 1977 Daytona 500 was essentially a tally of mechanical failures. Half of the field ended up in the garage or laps down due to breakdowns. Petty, Pearson, and Bobby Allison (running an American Motors Company factory–sponsored Matador) all dropped out of contention. Six cautions slowed the event, including a frightening, fiery crash on lap three. Bobby Wawak's Chevy broke its fuel line while at speed, and the car was engulfed in a fireball. Wawak frantically unbuckled and climbed out of the window of

the burning car while it was still rolling down the backstretch. Wawak didn't wait for the rescue crews but ran all the way to the infield care center, where he was treated for severe burns.

With the other front-runners out, the race came down to Benny Parsons (in his sixth season with L.G. DeWitt's No. 72 team) and Yarborough. Cale led the last thirty laps and became the only driver other than Richard Petty to win more than one Daytona 500 up to that time. It was a good start to the year, and Cale and the rest of the No. 11 team rode the momentum, repeating as Winston Cup champion.

LEFT: *Benny Parsons (left) gets some tips from the elder statesman of NASCAR, Lee Petty, before the 1977 running of the Daytona 500. Whatever Petty told him was gold—Parsons finished second, just behind the reigning Winston Cup champ, Cale Yarborough.*

ABOVE: *Ablaze in orange and red, the No. 11 Holly Farms crew celebrates Cale Yarborough's Daytona 500 win in 1977. It was Junior Johnson's third trip to Daytona 500 victory lane—once as a driver (1960) and twice as a car owner (1969 and 1977).*

OPPOSITE: *Coo Coo Marlin enjoys a quiet moment in the Daytona garage on July 1, 1975, during preparations for the Firecracker 400.*

Yarborough accomplished the near impossible in 1978 and became the only NASCAR driver ever to win three consecutive championships. Junior Johnson, along with many of the other GM teams, switched from Chevys to Oldsmobiles for Daytona and other superspeedway races, feeling that the sloped nose of the Olds gave teams an aerodynamic advantage over blockier makes.

Yarborough earned the pole for the race but couldn't hold off Bobby Allison (driving for ol' timer Bud Moore), who took the checkered flag. Buddy Baker again put in a strong showing and was leading with ten laps to go, but once more, the curse bit him and his engine let go. "What have I got to do to win? Man, I actually had a lap on the field and then this. I feel like crying," the big man lamented after the race.

The 1979 Daytona 500

The year 1979 marked the end of a proud tradition in NASCAR racing. Over the previous two years, NASCAR had been pushing teams to update their car models (normally a given model and year of car is run for three to four years). Dodge teams (Plymouth had dropped out by 1974) were still running the 1974 Charger model so were forced to switch. The only 1978 Dodge model that fit the NASCAR specs was the Magnum, and it turned out to be an unmitigated disaster. It was the beginning of the end for Mopar in NASCAR, and even long-time Chrysler stalwart Petty Enterprises switched to Chevys halfway through the year. So for 1979, Daytona was basically a Ford vs. GM race.

The biggest news at the start of the year was that CBS had decided to broadcast the 1979 Daytona 500 live, in its entirety. ABC had done well with its partial telecast of the 1976 event, but CBS was taking what most TV bigwigs thought was a sizable risk. The day started out with a scare for the network as rain fell at the track through the morning. Luckily, it stopped shortly before the scheduled start. To avoid a broadcast delay, NASCAR had the cars run fifteen or so laps under caution to dry the track.

Buddy Baker had captured yet another pole for the 500-miler (this time in Harry Ranier's No. 28 Olds), but it took less than forty laps this time before his engine expired and Baker was sitting dejectedly in the garage. The old familiar faces were at the front of the pack: Petty, Foyt, Darrell Waltrip, and Donnie Allison. A surprise leader was young Dale Earnhardt, son of old-time racer Ralph Earnhardt, in his first Daytona appearance. The racing was tight and it wasn't long before the first of seven caution flags appeared, as Cale Yarborough and Donnie Allison (in the No. 1 Hawaiian Tropic Olds) got tangled up. They collected Bobby Allison and the three cars slid into the muddy infield. The trio all went down a lap (Yarborough was down three) before they could get loose. They had fast cars, though, and by working the many cautions, they were able to make up

the deficits. Indeed, by lap 108 Donnie Allison had taken the lead. After swapping the point with Foyt and Earnhardt a couple of times, he started to pull away. And on his tail in second place was Cale Yarborough! The two drafted together over the last twenty laps and built up a sizable lead on third place. The finish would obviously be decided between the two of them.

They certainly did decide the finish, though not in the way anyone expected. As the pair ran nose to tail onto the backstretch for the final time, Yarborough swung to the inside to slingshot around Allison. Donnie had been waiting for the move, though, and moved down to block Cale. Yarborough didn't want to lose momentum so he kept moving down. Allison kept cutting left to block him. Pretty

BELOW: *A young Dale Earnhardt awaits the start of a race. Earnhardt's first serious ride was with Rod Osterlund. That team won a race in Dale's rookie season (1979) and followed up with a championship in only its second season (1980). Osterlund sold the venture to J.D. Stacy the next year, and the team quickly fell apart.*

soon they were into the grass, and Yarborough got loose and tagged No. 1. They bobbled together, looked like they would catch it, then slammed together again and headed up to the wall. As though joined, the two cars slid across the track and into the infield, coming to rest just a few feet apart in the grass.

As everyone watched in disbelief, Richard Petty and Darrell Waltrip suddenly realized they were racing for the lead. They streaked past the wrecked cars and on to the checkered flag, with Petty ahead by a car length to win his sixth Daytona 500.

As the CBS announcers sputtered in excitement over Petty's surprise win, Ken Squier cut in with, "There's a fight in turn three." Bobby Allison, who'd fallen laps down late in the event, stopped by to see if his brother Donnie needed any help. Yarborough was out of his car and on his way to chew on Donnie's ear for blocking him and vice versa for Allison. Bobby ended up in the middle of the ensuing brawl. The CBS cameras focused in on the fracas and showed the three fired-up racers slugging and kicking at each other in the mud. What a show!

The 1979 Daytona turned out to be a seminal event in NASCAR history. The sanctioning body publicly condemned the affair and penalized the participants, but had to be secretly pleased with the amount of attention the 500 and its postrace festivities brought to the sport. In addition, much of the eastern seaboard had been snowed in that day so viewership was through the roof. CBS execs were high-fiving all around as the race drew record ratings. NASCAR was suddenly big news all across the country.

NASCAR Downsizes

Since the oil embargo, Detroit had been downsizing its models to be more fuel-efficient. NASCAR was still running "boats" at the end of the 1970s, but handed out an ultimatum in 1980: it would be the final year the big models

BELOW: *Not a proud moment for the sport, but clearly an attention-getter. Bobby Allison grapples with Cale Yarborough's leg as Donnie Allison approaches the melee. This famous fracas took place following the last-lap crash in the 1979 Daytona 500 that took Cale and Donnie out of contention for the win.*

RIGHT: *Son Kyle joins Richard Petty in victory lane after the 1979 Daytona 500. Kyle's Winston Cup career began later that same year. The Petty and Earnhardt families are the only two to have won NASCAR Grand National and Winston Cup races over three generations.*

OPPOSITE: *Baker was so pumped up after his win in the 1980 Daytona 500 that he probably could have lifted the car if anyone had asked him to. Baker scored a total of five wins with Harry Ranier's No. 28 team in the 1979 and 1980 seasons.*

would be allowed. It was also the year that Buddy Baker finally made it to the checkered flag at Daytona. Baker again had the pole and led 143 laps on the way to his first Daytona 500 win. "I've been trying to win this race for twenty years!" laughed the victor.

Another fellow who would be echoing those words many years later had an outstanding day as well. Dale Earnhardt, on his way to a Winston Cup championship in only his second year, was in the lead late in the race and could have won it. Earnhardt's run was foiled by a black flag, assessed for missing lug nuts after the last pit stop. Also in the race but making her last appearance in NASCAR was USAC racer Janet Guthrie. She ran a companion car to Earnhardt's and finished eleventh—her best in a four-year run at stock car racing.

The year 1981 was a big one for the sport—or rather a small one, as it was the first season for the reduced-size models. Dodge tried to make a comeback with the Mirada but Richard Petty's test of the model immediately showed it to be a dud. That was the end for Mopar in NASCAR for quite a long time.

Most GM teams went with the Buick Regal for the year, and the statistics proved the decision was good one. Buick took twenty-two wins (its best year ever) in comparison to seven for Ford and one each for Chevy and Pontiac. The best-looking car at Speed Weeks wasn't the Buick, though, but a Pontiac LeMans. Harry Ranier's No. 28 LeMans,

with Bobby Allison at the wheel, was a standout and took the pole at 194.624 mph (313.217kph). Junior Johnson's No. 11 Buick (now with Darrell Waltrip driving) was the only other car even close. Allison won his qualifier handily and led over half the 500-miler, although tire strategy cost him the win. Richard Petty's No. 43 team went without new tires on the car's last pit stop, and the time saved put them ahead of Allison at the end. Petty got an unprecedented seventh Daytona 500 win!

All good things come to an end sooner or later. For the Pontiac LeMans, however,

LEFT: *Two generations of Allisons drove for Harry Ranier. Bobby piloted the No. 28 (seen here) during the 1981 season, winning five times. Son Davey drove for the team in 1987 and 1988 before it changed hands. Davey's pair of victories in his first full year was the record for rookie wins until Tony Stewart's amazing three-win 1999 debut season.*

OPPOSITE: *Among the most incredible of Richard Petty's racing records is his seven Daytona 500 wins. The 1981 victory was in a Buick, seen here with The King in victory lane.*

ABOVE: *Brothers Richard (center) and Maurice Petty (right) and cousin Dale Inman (left) were the brain trust of Petty Enterprises from 1961 onward and were responsible for the team's phenomenal success. Maurice took a turn at driving, but had more success as the engine builder/chief mechanic. Inman was the crew chief for the No. 43 team until the 1979 season, when he moved from an established champion to a future champion, Dale Earnhardt's No. 2 team.*

it was over right away. Rule changes on spoiler size reduced the competitiveness of the model, and the few Pontiac teams dropped it.

For more than thirty years, Petty Enterprises had been a winning team. Much of that was due to the skill of Lee and Richard Petty as drivers, but every bit as important were the top-notch cars and setups provided each week by crew chiefs Maurice Petty and Dale Inman. When Inman announced that he was leaving the team, right after winning the 1979 500, it rocked the Pettys' world. Whether due to that, struggles with new models of cars, or King Richard's ongoing health problems, from that time on the wins dwindled, with the last at Daytona in July 1984 at the Pepsi Firecracker 400. The seventh Daytona 500 win in 1981 would be the last.

With Buddy Baker finally winning the Great American Race in 1980, Darrell Waltrip took over the leading role as the "guy who couldn't catch a break" at Daytona.

Faster and Faster

Speeds on the circuit's fastest tracks had pretty well leveled out over the years after the aero wars. By the late 1970s, though, they were again on the rise, and safety would once more become the sport's biggest concern.

Speeds started climbing in 1979. Buddy Baker's pole run that year was more than 196 mph (315.4kph), a big jump from the 187 mph (300.9kph) of the previous year. As teams adjusted to the new, smaller cars, the speeds hovered in that range until 1983, when Cale Yarborough broke the magic barrier with a qualifying speed at Daytona of

84   THE MODERN ERA

201.84 mph (324.83kph). Then came 1985, when the barrier completely dissolved.

That year, "Awesome" Bill Elliott and his home-grown Georgia family team showed the stock car world that people didn't know yet what "fast" was. The Elliotts beat the system a bit by narrowing the width of their sleek new Ford T-Bird (a parameter not then covered in the NASCAR rulebook), and the No. 9 Coors cars cut through the wind at Daytona and Talladega faster than any stock car ever had or would. Bill ran 205 mph (329.9kph) at Daytona and 209 mph (336.3kph) at Talladega. Then, when the other teams thought they had caught up, he upped the ante to 212.229 mph (341.549kph) in the Winston 500 in May 1986. The *pièce de résistance* was his 1987 Winston 500 run, with a pole speed of 212.809 mph (342.483kph).

Where would the dizzying upward spiral end? Well, it almost ended in tragedy in the grandstands at Talladega during that 1987 race. The Winston Cup cars were carefully designed to slice through the air at high speeds, as long as they were going forward. If they turned around at those speeds, though, they turned into kites that would suddenly lift into the air, flip over, and tumble in terrifying crashes. In the May 1987 Talladega race, Bobby Allison's Buick spun along the front stretch with a blown tire. The car became airborne and hit the fence, tearing down 150 feet (45.6m) of the wire. Debris shredded through the crowd and several spectators were injured. It was great luck that the car tumbled back down to the track rather than into the stands through the rent in the fence, but it still scared the life out of everyone in the sport. NASCAR acted quickly to curb the speeds at Daytona and Talladega, and beginning in 1988, racing there changed dramatically.

BELOW: *Joe Ruttman (No. 98) and Geoffrey Bodine (No. 50) swerve to avoid the spinning Pepsi Chevy of Darrell Waltrip. Waltrip's No. 11 slammed into the inside retaining wall in this 1983 Daytona 500 crash, knocking the two-time champion unconscious. Waltrip sustained a concussion from the accident, and the championship points that Bobby Allison (who finished in the top ten) gained on him that day ultimately helped Allison to finally defeat "Jaws" (after three years of trying) in the Winston Cup title chase.*

ABOVE: *In 1982, Kentucky coal magnate Jim Stacy set his sights on the Winston Cup series. Stacy fielded two teams himself and sponsored five others (including one with Dave Marcis, shown here) at the start of the season. By October, though, Stacy was having financial difficulties, and the sponsorship and team monies dried up. He was down to one team for 1983, then disappeared from the sport as suddenly as he had arrived.*

GM Back on Top

By 1980, NASCAR was prominent enough to attract the attention of a number of "big money men" who tried their hands at team or track ownership. J.D. (Jim) Stacy was one such man, and certainly one-of-a-kind. Stacy took the Carl Keikhafer approach to team ownership in 1982, at least in terms of numbers, and had his name plastered on no fewer than seven cars in the Daytona 500. Stacy's NASCAR empire was built on shaky financial grounds, though, and he closed up shop at the end of the 1983 season with just one NASCAR win.

Bobby Allison was thwarted in his 1981 bid for victory at Daytona, but with a little luck and a new team, he pulled it off the next year. The DiGard Buick didn't look like a favorite at first. In fact, just four laps into the race, the rear bumper fell off the car. That turned out to be just what the doctor ordered! Wind tunnel testing showed that cars actually ran quicker at Daytona without the bumper (less drag), and Allison proved them right, taking the lead on lap fifteen and spending most of the afternoon there. Allison won the race, his very first run in the DiGard ride. Competitors cried foul

after the event, accusing Allison's crew chief, Gary Nelson, of rigging the bumper to drop off. It probably didn't help that Nelson was known as a creative innovator who wasn't afraid to bend the rules a bit. Nelson later became the chief technical inspector for NASCAR (on the principle that it takes a thief to catch a thief).

For many years, the road race at Riverside, California, had been the first race of the NASCAR season. Starting in 1983, that event moved to the summer, and the Daytona 500 took its current place as the leadoff race for the year.

At the beginning of the 1980s, Cale Yarborough had decided to cut back his racing schedule. Despite lucrative offers to go for the championship, he ran only selected events for the rest of his career. Yarborough had moved to the Ranier No. 28 team in 1983, and though he wasn't running for the points that year or the next, he sure was running fast at Daytona. The veteran was on his way to a pole-qualifying lap in 1983 when he tumbled his car. Ricky Rudd (in Richard Childress' No. 3) inherited the top spot. Ranier rolled out a backup Pontiac for the Sunday race, and it proved to be strong enough. Yarborough pulled his patented last lap slingshot on leader Buddy Baker and took the checkered flag.

Yarborough had a special passenger in the cockpit with him for that race. CBS installed an in-car camera at his back. Larry Frank had

carried a movie camera in his Holman-Moody Ford way back in the 1963 Daytona 500, but Yarborough's was the first live feed to the TV audience.

Yarborough was "on a rail" again for the 1984 February classic, and he turned in a blistering lap of 201.848 mph (324.843kph) for the pole. He ran up front for most of the event and again put himself in position to make a last lap pass for the lead. This time it was Darrell Waltrip who watched the No. 28 (Chevy, that year) slingshot by to take the most important lap—the last one.

ABOVE: *Vice President George Bush waves the green flag to start the 1983 Daytona 500. Since the time when former President Jimmy Carter had invited NASCAR stars to the White House in 1978, many of the nation's senior executives have attended races at Daytona. The Daytona Beach Airport sits just off the track's backstretch, affording easy access (and egress) for Air Force One.*

LEFT: *Despite having cut back in his racing activities in the early 1980s, Cale Yarborough was one of the toughest competitors at Daytona in 1983 and 1984. He won the event in dramatic fashion, in both instances coming from the number two spot on the last lap to win the race. Here, Yarborough's No. 28 takes the checkered flag on February 19, 1984.*

Independence Day at Daytona

Joe Weatherly's performance in the 1961 race is worth noting. He only managed a sixth-place finish, but that wasn't bad considering the circumstances. His gear shifter wouldn't stay engaged and he had to drive the race with his right leg wrapped around the lever, using only his left foot for the gas, brake, and clutch pedals. It was Fireball Roberts' year at Daytona in 1962—he won all three races he ran at the track that year. He again won the July race in 1963, his last running of that event.

EVERY YEAR SINCE 1959 there's been a second major points race held at Daytona International Speedway. It was originally run to fill the void in the schedule left when USAC pulled out of a planned Daytona race, but has become an important stop on the circuit and has hosted some of the series' most exciting finishes. The race started out as the "Firecracker 250." Over the years, the race length changed, and in 1987, Pepsi signed on as a sponsor. Since then, it's been known as the Pepsi 400.

Surprisingly, the summer race is quite dissimilar from the Daytona 500. It's a shorter event, and, as we've seen, quite a bit can change during that last 100 miles (160.9km). The weather conditions are quite different as well. The track and air temperatures are much higher (we're talking July in Florida), so the setups from the February classic do not apply.

Fireball Roberts couldn't seem to win the Daytona 500 but immediately conquered the Firecracker 250, taking the first running of that race in 1959 from the pole. "Tiger" Tom Pistone thought he could snooker the speedy No. 22 by making one fewer pit stop for gas, but the strategy backfired on him when he ran dry on lap forty-eight.

The summer race at Daytona has turned up a few surprise and first-time winners over the years. Sam McQuagg got his first and only NASCAR win there in 1966, running a Dodge Charger equipped with a rear deck spoiler to give him a bit of a handling edge. LeeRoy Yarbrough's team also used a mechanical innovation to win the 1969 event. Instead of running the exhaust pipes out the side of the car, as usual, they moved them to the rear. Any car that tried to draft up on Yarbrough

OPPOSITE: *Richard Petty celebrates his 200th win, in the 1984 Firecracker 400. Some felt that it should have been win number 199, in fact: Petty was cited for major tire and engine rules violations after his victory at Charlotte the previous October, which could easily have resulted in disqualification of the win. NASCAR did fine the team heavily, but let the win stand. Even so, it cast a bit of a shadow over Petty's record.*

BELOW: *The 1966 Firecracker 400 was the first race for Sam McQuagg (shown here in the garage) since the same event two years earlier. He put his Ray Nichels Dodge at the front early in the race and kept it there for most of the afternoon, making McQuagg a surprise winner.*

soon found its engine overheating as the exhaust from No. 26 blew right into the trailing car's grille.

With the dawning of the modern era, the July race was lengthened to 400 miles (643.7km). The format appeared to be designed just for David Pearson, who won the event from 1972 to 1974 and again in 1978.

Perhaps the most exciting Firecracker 400 was in 1984. President Ronald Reagan was on hand for the finish of the race and watched Richard Petty and Cale Yarborough banging doors at 200 mph (321.8kph) for the win. Both drivers had won the race before, but this one had the potential to be a bit special. Richard Petty had 199 wins at the time and cherished the thought of picking up number 200 while the president was there. (Petty is a long-standing Republican supporter.) With three laps left, a caution flew for a crash in turn one, and the

two cars set up to battle back to the flag. They raced down the front chute door to door, and Petty edged Yarborough out by less than a foot (.3m). Yarborough should have finished second, but in the anticlimax of the caution laps, he had pulled into the pits one lap shy of the finish. It's a favorite bit of NASCAR trivia: Harry Gant thus finished second to Petty on his two hundredth win, even though it had been Yarborough who had made the race so thrilling.

Greg Sacks joined Sam McQuagg as a dark-horse winner by taking the 1985 race. Sacks was in a DiGard R&D (research and development) car and beat out the team's main entry, Bobby Allison.

Dale Earnhardt's Daytona curse apparently didn't extend to the July race. Dale won two of the races, in 1990 and 1993. Earnhardt's was one of the few cars left in the 1990 race after a

twenty-four car crash decimated the field. Geoffey Bodine blamed the crash on the movie, released earlier that year, *Days of Thunder.* The film was about stock car racing but inaccurately depicted drivers deliberately wrecking each other to gain position.

"Mr. Excitement," Jimmy Spencer, gave fans the most exciting finish of the first half of the 1994 season in the Pepsi 400. Spencer had never won a race but hooked up with a solid Junior Johnson team sponsored by McDonald's. The only lap he led in the race was the last one, passing, then holding off, Ernie Irvan by a hair to take the checkered flag. Spencer backed his performance up with a win later that same month at Talladega.

Two more first-time winners, the driver and team owner, took the 1997 event. John Andretti was on the team of Cale Yarborough (who'd had much less success as a car owner than as a driver) and put the No. 98 RCA Ford in victory lane after an

outstanding run. Andretti has had some more success with Petty Enterprises since, but it remains the Yarborough team's only win.

The 1998 Pepsi 400 had to be postponed, not for rain, as is usually the case, but because of fire. Severe brushfires had plagued Florida and came close enough to the track to necessitate canceling the event. With the expansion of the NASCAR schedule, the first open date was months later in October. Daytona International Speedway management had a treat in store for the fans when the race was finally held. They had installed a lighting system at the big track, and the Pepsi 400 was run at night. It was an incredible undertaking, and the results were spectacular. Jeff Gordon was in the zone that year, and the night race was his eleventh win of the season (by the end of which he had tied Richard Petty's modern-era record of thirteen wins).

Owner Jack Roush finally got a Daytona win in the third running of the night race in 2000. Jeff Burton broke the team's restrictor plate jinx after a judicious two-tire stop put him ahead near the end of the race.

The 1985 Daytona 500

The relationship between NASCAR and the R.J. Reynolds tobacco company had been successful but by the mid-1980s had still not brought what both parties hoped for: national recognition of the Winston Cup series. In 1985, the sponsor came up with a program that they felt would quickly change that.

It was called the "Winston Million," a one-million-dollar prize to be paid out to any driver who could win any three out of four selected races in a season. The races included the Daytona 500 (the most prestigious race), the Winston 500 (the fastest race), the World 600 (the longest race), and the Southern 500 (the oldest race). Collect the winner's trophy at any three of those, and RJR would pay out a cool million, in addition to the normal race-prize money. A consolation prize of $100,000 would be awarded to the driver(s) who won two of the four.

The criterion for the award was carefully chosen. It certainly seemed attainable; many drivers had won more than three races in a season. However, looking back through the statistics showed that only LeeRoy Yarbrough and David Pearson had ever won any three of those events in the same year. So while the program had big publicity power, the tobacco

company wasn't concerned that it would have to make the payout any time soon.

They hadn't counted on "Awesome" Bill Elliott, though. The No. 9 team, owned by industrialist Harry Melling, put together a dream year and astounded the racing world. Their odyssey started at Daytona in February.

Cale Yarborough set the qualifying bar higher than ever before by nailing a lap at 203.814 mph (328.006kph). Five other drivers exceeded 200, but Yarborough was the class of the field. Until, that is, the No. 9 Coors Ford hit the track. Bill Elliott gritted his teeth and ran a time that set everyone back on their heels. The redhead wrote the record at 205.114 mph (330.099kph).

It wasn't a fluke lap, either; Elliott backed it up with a win in the 125-mile (201.1km) qualifier, pulling away from the field with ease to lead forty-eight of the fifty laps, none at slower than 197 mph (317kph). "The handwriting is on the wall," lamented Darrell Waltrip, who finished second to Elliott—just a few car lengths from being a lap down. Not everyone was willing to concede the race, though, and the wily veteran Yarborough, who won his own qualifier, thought he'd be able to contest the Georgian.

It looked like he might be right, as Cale led many of the first fifty laps of the 500-miler. Then on lap sixty-two, his engine let go, and there was no one left who had a prayer of catching the No. 9 car. Elliott kept the pace at 192 mph (308.9kph) through the first 100 miles (160.9km), and the strain of trying to keep up with the pace he set started compromising the other cars' engines.

The only chance the competition really had was on a penalty to the No. 9 team. After their last pit stop, officials called the red rocket back in again to fix an errant headlight panel cover. Even with the extra stop, Elliott retook the lead in only eleven laps. The last caution of the day provided at least some excitement for the finish. With only one lap to go, Elliott and Lake Speed (the only other driver still on the lead lap) took off nose to tail. Speed had a shot at an upset win, but not much of one. Elliott pulled away steadily through the final lap to win by one second.

The No. 9 team continued to dominate superspeedway events through the year, and Elliott won the Winston 500, the second leg of the Winston Million in dramatic fashion, making up a full two-lap deficit under green. The team was dogged by problems at Charlotte, though, so his Million chance came down to the Southern 500 at Darlington. As though predestined, Elliott avoided crashes and fought

LEFT: *With the more recent success of Jeff Gordon, it is sometimes forgotten that Geoffrey Bodine was the driver who brought Rick Hendrick's race teams to prominence in the 1980s. There were no championships during that period, but Bodine won five races with the No. 5 team, including the 1986 Daytona 500. Bodine and family are shown here celebrating that win in victory lane.*

BELOW LEFT: *The start of the 1986 Daytona 500. Eight caution flags flew in the event, and a quarter of the race was run under yellow. Crashes took out such solid contenders as Richard Petty, Cale Yarborough, Buddy Baker, and Harry Gant. Mechanical failures further depleted the field to just more than half of the starting number by the end.*

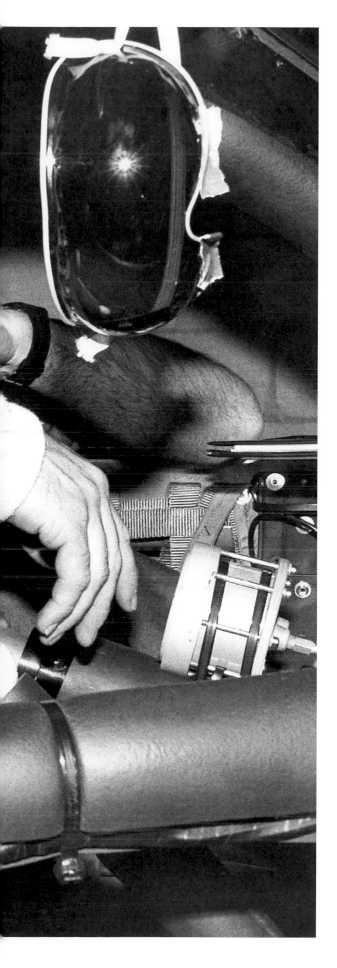

back from problems while the top contenders fell. "Awesome" Bill that day became "Million Dollar" Bill, and R.J. Reynolds paid out the biggest racing prize ever in its very first offering.

The first year that there wasn't a Petty Enterprises car in the field of a Daytona 500 was 1985. Both Richard and his son, Kyle, were there, but Kyle was in the Wood Brothers No. 21, and Richard had moved to Mike Curb Motorsports with his signature No. 43 for 1984 and 1985.

Elliott on the Move

The No. 9 crew wasn't able to convert its superspeedway dominance to the 1985 Winston Cup championship, but they were still the team to beat on pole qualifying day through 1986 and 1987. Bill ran another 205 mph (329.9kph) lap for the 1986 Daytona 500 front spot and won his qualifier. He wasn't really a factor in the Sunday race, though. He fell back into the pack and was taken out by a multicar crash halfway through the event. Rick Hendrick Motorsports captured its first Daytona 500 trophy that year with Geoffrey Bodine behind the wheel of the No. 5 Chevy. Dale Earnhardt was racing second to Bodine in the closing laps and just waiting for his chance, but his Richard Childress Chevy ran dry with three laps left, and Dale had to pit for gas.

The series underwent a simple but significant change at the beginning of 1986. NASCAR's premier league would no longer be known as the Grand National Winston Cup. The name was shortened, to emphasize R.J. Reynold's involvement, to just The Winston Cup. Surprisingly, it took many years for sports writers and fans to warm up to the change. The Grand National title shifted over to NASCAR's "bush league," (sponsored by Anheuser-Busch beer), which came to be called the Busch Grand National series.

Bill Elliott's 1987 Daytona pole speed was an astounding 210.364 mph (338.548kph), which is still the record. That year, it was Bodine's turn to run out of gas in a late-race gamble, and Elliott, who had led more than half of the laps already, won his second Daytona 500.

LEFT: *A portrait of one of the most successful teams in Winston Cup racing. Dale Earnhardt (left) goes over his concerns with car owner Richard Childress (center) and crew chief Kirk Shelmerdine (right) before the 1987 Daytona race. That was the last year the team sported the blue and yellow Wrangler colors. They finished fifth at Daytona but won eleven other events and notched their second championship (Earnhardt's third).*

Chapter Four

RESTRICTOR PLATES

IT WAS A WHOLE DIFFERENT STORY IN 1988. Winston Cup teams faced two significant new challenges that year as they prepared for the Daytona 500 in February.

The first was the reinstitution of carburetor restrictor plates for the races at Daytona and Talladega superspeedways. After Bobby Allison's harrowing crash at the Alabama track in 1987, NASCAR decided to slow the cars by requiring the use of a plate at the two fastest superspeedways. Restrictor plates restrict the inflow of air to an engine's combustion chamber and reduce the horsepower generated. Teams found that they needed to start up restrictor plate engine programs to find ways to optimize the specific power plants used just for those races. Some teams adapted well while others that were always strong at other big tracks (e.g., the Jack Roush and Roger Penske teams) have yet to find the secret to winning at the restrictor plate venues.

ABOVE: *A recent aerial view of the Daytona International Speedway. Lake Lloyd is a favorite spot for boating and fishing during Speed Weeks, but at least one driver visited the lake in his car during a race: Tommy Irwin had to be fished out of the pond after a crash in the 1960 Daytona qualifier.*

LEFT: *Daytona is one of the NASCAR venues where both Busch Grand National and Winston Cup races are held on the same weekend. For years, Winston Cup drivers have run in the corresponding Busch races to get a feel for the track before the main event. In fact, Mark Martin, a Winston Cup driver, holds the record for the most wins in the BGN series. Here, a crash blocks the track during the 1990 Goody's 300 Busch race.*

For the drivers, the use of restrictor plates completely changed the dynamics of racing at those tracks over the subsequent years. The plates took the top end off of the horsepower curve, evening out the speed of the competitors. Plate races became characterized by long "freight trains" of cars—sometimes the entire field—all packed together nose to tail and side by side.

Drafting became the critical factor in gaining or losing positions, with long strings of cars having the aerodynamic advantage over a single car or pair of cars. Drivers stay in the draft, hoping that their "cash register line" will advance more quickly than the others and bring them to the front. If a driver does break out to pass, he'd better hope he has friends in the field to go with him because a single car out of line goes straight to the back. It's "Chutes and Ladders" at 190 mph (305.7kph). In the 1970s, second place was the place to be on the last lap—ready to execute a slingshot move around the leader. With restrictor plates, cars rarely have the over-the-top horsepower to pull off that move, and must rely on help from drafting partners to push them ahead. To be competitive, drivers must not only pass the test of racing just inches apart in a

pack with forty other cars, but they must excel at the complicated chess game of drafting.

Restrictor plate racing is also fraught with danger. With that many cars that close together, one slip can take out half of the field. They call those crashes "the Big One," and every driver fears being caught up in it.

The year 1988 was also the first time in many years that NASCAR faced a tire war. The Hoosier Tire Company felt it had a compound to challenge Goodyear (NASCAR's sole rubber supplier since the late 1960s) and convinced a number of teams to go with its tires. Neil Bonnett finished fourth in the Daytona 500 with Hoosiers, and at the next race, at Richmond, Morgan Shepherd put Hoosiers on the pole. The company scored several wins through the first half of the year, and marginal teams started looking at the new tires as a way to pull off a rare victory.

The competition between the companies undoubtedly resulted in faster, more cutting-edge tires, but it was a double-edged sword. With only Goodyear in the pool for many years, the trend had been toward safer rather than faster tires. Since all teams used the same brand, how fast the tires were had been a non-factor in competition. As both companies pushed faster formulas, however, blowouts and injuries from tire failure became a problem.

Hoosier tires put up a stiff fight, but the small Indiana firm was no match for Goodyear in the long run. By the middle of the season, most teams had decided they weren't willing to take a chance on the new brand. Citing the safety concerns, Hoosier voluntarily dropped out of the series—a class move on the part of owner Bob Newton.

The 1988 Daytona 500: A Family Affair

There have been many family acts in NASCAR racing over the years, so it was no surprise when Bobby Allison's son Davey joined him on the Winston Cup circuit. Davey proved a quick study and was the first driver to win two races in his rookie year (1987). The two drivers affirmed the human side of the sport and gave stock car racing one of its most memorable moments when Bobby jumped out of his car to dash to his son's aid after a fiery crash in a Busch Grand National race.

Bobby was in his fourth year with the Stavola Brothers team in 1988 (having moved from the crumbling DiGard operation partway through the 1985 season) and piloted the gold and white No. 12 Miller High Life Buick. Davey had hooked up with Harry Ranier's No. 28 Texaco team and helped convince master engine builder Robert Yates to take over the reins when Ranier bowed out later in 1988. Both Allisons had strong cars for the Florida race and scored second- (Davey) and third-place (Bobby) starting spots. Ken Schrader put

Rick Hendrick's No. 25 Chevy on the pole at a sedate 193.829 mph (311.937kph), almost 17 mph (27.3kph) slower than Elliott's 1987 run, thanks to the carburetor plates.

Several drivers ran up front that day with Bobby Allison and Darrell Waltrip evenly splitting the most laps led. Waltrip was out front with about twenty to go when the Daytona monkey climbed up on his back and his engine went sour. He faded to an eleventh-place finish. Davey Allison slid around Phil Parsons (younger brother of 1973 champ Benny) a few laps later and pulled No. 28 along with him into second. Father and son carried on a spirited battle over the dwindling laps, with Bobby edging out the win by two car lengths.

BELOW: *After incidental contact, the No. 43 spun on the front stretch during the 1988 Daytona 500. A.J. Foyt touched the car as it was spinning and Petty's Pontiac lifted up off the ground and went into an aerial tumble against the catch fence. Preventing this type of crash was the idea behind requiring restrictor plates for cars at Daytona and Talladega.*

It isn't very often that the second-place finisher is as happy as the winner, but Davey had no complaints after following dad across the line. For Bobby, it was a glimpse of good things to come. He said, "It was a great feeling to look back and see someone you think is the best coming-up driver and know it's your son." It was the first father-son, 1-2 finish since Lee and Richard Petty's at Heidelberg, Pennsylvania, in 1960.

Unfortunately, Richard Petty wasn't around to offer congratulations to the pair—he'd been involved in a horrifying crash on lap 106. Petty traded paint a bit with Phil Barkdoll and went into a spin. The rear of the car lifted and No. 43 tumbled down the front straight, against the retaining wall. A half-dozen end-over-end rolls left nothing but the cockpit cage, which took a final hard shot as Brett Bodine ran head-on into

it. Amazingly, Petty suffered only an ankle sprain in the accident.

Davey went on to two wins of his own that year, but it was the last of eighty-five in Bobby Allison's career. Later that summer, at Pocono, the elder Allison was T-boned on the driver's side at full speed by another car, and the 1983 champ was gravely injured. Allison's career was over and he faced a long recovery. He was left with permanent memory loss as well, which robbed him of his and Davey's day in the sun that year at Daytona.

Tell Me This Is The Daytona 500!

Darrell Waltrip had not won the Daytona 500 since he had started trying in 1972. Over the seventeen years up to 1989, he'd won a ton of races and three championships and had been in Daytona's victory lane five times for qualifer wins, but never for the big prize.

Waltrip started on the outside of the front row in 1989, but wasn't one of the fastest cars in the race. His Hendrick teammates Geoffrey Bodine and Ken Schrader had two of the better cars, and it looked like Schrader was on his way to his second Winston Cup win and a coveted Daytona trophy. Ol' D.W. has been known over the years as a crafty racer when it comes to gas mileage, though, and decided, with crew chief Jeff Hammond (now a FOX NASCAR announcer), to forego the last pit stop for fuel. When Schrader, Bodine, and others pulled onto pit road for a splash-and-go, Waltrip inherited the lead, taking his teammates to a 1-2-3 Hendrick sweep running on fumes. They had cut it close—the car shut off, out of gas, on the way to victory lane!

Always a ham, Waltrip clowned and danced in the winner's circle. "I won the Daytona 500!" he exclaimed, then paused as though in horror: "This is the Daytona 500, isn't it? Please tell me this *is* the Daytona 500?"

ABOVE: *Father and son enjoy the traditional winner's shower (though, in this case, with Miller beer) in victory lane after Bobby Allison (right) won the 1988 Daytona 500.*

LEFT: *Darrell Waltrip does an impromptu version of the "Ickey Shuffle" (a victory dance made famous at the time by Cincinnati Bengals running back Ickey Woods) after winning the 1989 Daytona 500. Waltrip won the race on fuel mileage, not the first or last time he pulled off that trick. In fact, his last career win as a driver (the 1992 Southern 500) came as a result of making one less fuel stop than did his competitors.*

ABOVE: *The 1990 Daytona 500 was a Cinderella story for the Bob Whitcomb No. 10 team. Whitcomb had fielded cars for Ken Bouchard and Derrike Cope since 1988 without even a top-five finish. The 1990 Daytona win, with Cope at the wheel of the No. 10, and a follow-up victory in Dover later that year, established the team as a contender on the circuit.*

New Contenders

The losing-Daytona buck passed immediately to Dale Earnhardt once Waltrip won the 1989 event. Earnhardt had already had several sound runs at a 500 and been foiled. From 1990 on, though, he really got serious about finding creative ways to lose the race.

The black No. 3 was head and shoulders above the field for the 1990 race. Earnhardt started in second (Ken Schrader won his third straight Daytona 500 pole—every one since restrictor plates) and left the field in his dust in the big race. Heading into the last laps, he had a comfortable margin over a surprisingly strong Derrike Cope (running in the Day-Glo red and white Purolator Chevy). Earnhardt took the white flag, then, as he headed into turn two, it happened. Running over something on the track (allegedly a chicken bone thrown by a fan), Earnhardt lost a tire. He hung on down the backstretch, but it blew wide open in turn three and he slowed and slid up the banking.

An astounded Cope darted under him and led Terry Labonte around to the checkered flag and his first win.

The 1991 Daytona could have been anyone's race. Davey Allison stepped up as the new leader of the Alabama Gang and took the pole and first qualifier race. Earnhardt, Allison, and Kyle Petty were the front-runners, though Californian Ernie Irvan, in his second year with the Morgan-McClure Kodak team, led as well.

Nine cautions mixed up the field quite a bit. There was a change in pit rules that year; cars had to stay under a certain speed limit (which varied by track) on pit road. The rule came after a crewmember was pinned and killed by a car sliding out of control on the team's pit road entrance. Teams were wary of the extra time they would lose on green-flag pit stops and stretched their runs as long as possible, wearing out tires.

With ten laps to go, Kyle Petty slipped up into Rusty Wallace and triggered a crash that took out those two, Waltrip, and others.

Earnhardt emerged from the pits first and was ready to take off at the green flag, but Irvan skunked him on the restart and grabbed the lead. Davey Allison pulled up beside No. 3 to battle for second, and as the two fought, Earnhardt's worn tires let him down. His rear end slid up into Allison and the two crashed. There were only two laps left, so it looked like the race would end under caution and Irvan (in third place at the time) would have a win.

It wasn't quite over, though. Irvan's car had developed a fuel pickup problem, and it started cutting out as they toured the banking at slow speeds. Sterling Marlin followed closely, hoping Irvan would sputter to a stop on the last yellow flag lap, but Irvan kept No. 4 down on the apron and hung in for the victory.

There was a special set of cars in the 1991 Daytona race to pay respect to the U.S. Armed Forces engaged at the time in Operation Desert

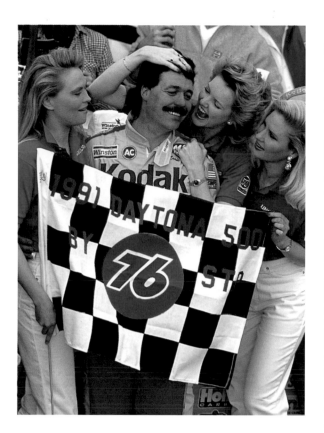

Shield. R.J. Reynolds backed five otherwise unsponsored teams and painted their cars with the colors of the U.S. Army, Navy, Air Force, Coast Guard, and Marines. Alan Kulwicki's No. 7 Army Ford particularly stood out. The tan, olive, and black camouflage paint scheme was—well, ugly—but it caught everyone's attention and helped draw a more permanent sponsor for the under-appreciated driver.

Davey Allison stayed out of trouble in the 1992 race, avoiding "the Big One," a crash that took out fourteen cars on lap ninety two, and the Allisons joined the Pettys as the only father-son winners of the Great American Race. Bill Elliott, after several unsuccessful seasons, had left the No. 9 team to join Junior Johnson's No. 11 operation. Elliott and stablemate Sterling Marlin were the quality cars early on. After a crash on lap eighty-four, the two resumed the lead but were joined up front by Ernie Irvan. Irvan had acquired a reputation over the previous few seasons as a talented but overly aggressive driver ("Swervin' Irvan"), so when he went three-wide with the Johnson cars, everyone held their breath. Then it happened. The crash wasn't really anyone's fault, just too many cars in too little space, but thirteen cars were caught up in the mess. Allison picked his way through the wreckage and held off Morgan Shepherd (in the Wood Brothers' No. 21) to take the win.

NASCAR paid its farewells to two giants of the sport that year. Richard Petty had announced that 1992 would be his last year as a driver, so that was the last of his thirty-two Daytona

500s. In June, "Big Bill" France, visionary and father of the sport, passed away in his Ormond Beach, Florida, home. "The Tall Man" had been seriously ill, and away from NASCAR operations for several years, but his death left a void impossible to fill.

The 1993 Daytona 500: The "Dale and Dale Show"

It had become a yearly question: "Will Dale Earnhardt finally win the Daytona 500?" And each year, he looked strong enough to pull it off. Earnhardt won the second qualifier for the No. 3 team in 1993, but there were some different faces in the front three starting spots.

Kyle Petty, in Felix Sabates's No. 42 Mello Yello car, took the pole, and Dale Jarrett earned his first Daytona front row start. Jarrett had joined a new team in 1992, run by Super Bowl–winning football coach Joe Gibbs.

Starting second was rookie driver Jeff Gordon, fresh from the Busch Grand National ranks and teamed up in a Rick Hendrick Chevy

ABOVE: *Fans and friends say farewell to a legend. The 1992 Daytona 500 was the last in Richard Petty's career as a racer. Petty had run in thirty-three of the thirty-four events to that date—he missed the 1965 race when Chrysler boycotted the series— and won more than a fifth of those.*

OPPOSITE: *Some observers in the NASCAR garage doubted Dale Jarrett's ability to run at the championship level. Jarrett demonstrated his winning potential with the new Joe Gibbs No. 18 team, in 1993 and 1994. His 1993 Daytona 500 win had come down to a head-to-head duel with the best in the business—Dale Earnhardt—and left no doubt that the younger Jarrett could drive a race car.*

with crew chief Ray Evernham. Gordon and the No. 24 team immediately showed there was more to the team than hype by winning the first 125-mile (201.1km) qualifier.

There was another Hendrick car running in the qualifier as well. Indy Car champ Al Unser Jr. was trying his hand at a Daytona stock car race. Unser dropped out after losing a tire and hitting the wall, although he made the Sunday race based on his qualifying time.

Jeff Gordon was eager to run up front on Sunday and shot around Petty to lead lap one. Jarrett, Petty, Earnhardt, Schrader, and others (thirteen different drivers in total) swapped the lead back and forth in the typical restrictor plate shuffle, but it was the No. 3 team that clearly had the car to beat. Petty had a car that might challenge, but he was taken out in a crash after Earnhardt and Unser Jr. (who had put on an impressive charge through the field) got together. It wouldn't be the last time over the years that those two would lock bumpers, and their rivalry added excitement to many IROC (International Race of Champions) races.

Where was the other front row starter? Jarrett had led a few laps near the start of the race but faded to mid-pack through most of the race. As the afternoon wore on, though, Jarrett made his

RESTRICTOR PLATES

way back to the front. Hooking up in a draft with Geoffrey Bodine, he broke out of the main pack and tracked down the lead group. The final caution flag flew on lap 168 when Michael Waltrip (Darrell's younger brother) and Derrike Cope crashed. Rusty Wallace was caught up, and his No. 2 Pontiac went sideways and then starting rolling. A dozen somersaults later Rusty emerged from the wreckage with only a cut on his chin.

On the restart, Earnhardt lined up first, followed by Bodine, Jarrett, Gordon, and the McDonald's Ford of Hut Stricklin. With a handful of laps to go, it again looked like Dale had the right stuff. But there were two Dales in that pack, and it was the other one—Jarrett—who started making the moves. Jarrett slid his No. 18 Chevy around Jeff Gordon on the high side and lined up to go after the lead with two circuits left. Going into turn three, Earnhardt got a touch loose, letting Jarrett slide

up under him, and the front four lined up two by two for the white flag lap.

Jeff Gordon tucked in behind Dale (Earnhardt), and Bodine followed Dale (Jarrett). Stricklin, still in fifth, split the difference, waiting to see which line would give him an advantage. They were dead even under the flag stand, but Jarrett got a bump from Bodine that pushed him ahead as they roared into turn one for the last time. He took the lead and slid up in front of Earnhardt going down the backstretch.

Adding a touch of warmth to the final laps was the CBS broadcast of the finish. Two-time Grand National champ Ned Jarrett was in the broadcast booth and calling the race. Ned, Dale Jarrett's father, called the laps as though he were coaching his son from the pit box. "Stay low, don't let him get under you—that's it!" he instructed as Jarrett swerved side to side down the backstretch and into turn three to

hold off the determined Earnhardt. Jarrett ran the perfect line through those final turns and took the checkered flag 0.16 seconds ahead of No. 3. "Dale Jarrett's won the Daytona 500!" announced the proud papa to the viewing audience. There wasn't a dry eye in the house.

It was the "Dale and Dale Show," but Dale Earnhardt once again came out on the short end. "Big damn deal, I lost another Daytona 500," the disgruntled racer spat as he was trailed by the media to his hauler after the race.

Marlin Steps Up

NASCAR was haunted by tragedy later in 1993 and lost two of its brightest young stars. The 1992 champion, Alan Kulwicki (beating out Bill Elliott in the last laps of the last race by the tightest points margin ever), was killed in April when the small plane carrying him and executives from his sponsor, Hooter's Restaurants, crashed on its way to Bristol Speedway. The enigmatic engineer-turned-racer had only a brief few months to enjoy his championship.

Then in July, Davey Allison was killed when the helicopter he was piloting flipped over as he came in to land at Talladega Superspeedway to watch a test session. The Allisons had lost younger son Clifford in a racing accident earlier that year, too, so Davey's death was a crippling blow. Dale Earnhardt won the race at Pocono the following week and demonstrated the solidarity of the racing community by paying tribute to the two heroes. Earnhardt drove a Kulwicki-style "Polish victory lap" (once the wrong way around the track) while holding a flag saluting Allison's No. 28.

In 1994 Ernie Irvan had taken over Allison's seat in Robert Yates' Ford, and Sterling Marlin filled the consequently vacated No. 4 Kodak ride. These turned out to be good moves for both men.

The Hoosier Tire Company was back in the picture that year with a new, improved compound. Rookie Loy Allen startled the garage by taking the Daytona pole on Hoosiers, but there wouldn't be any teams running them in the 500-

miler itself. Neil Bonnett had been testing a new car for his racing comeback (he'd suffered head injuries several years earlier) and was running on Hoosier tires. As he entered the tri-oval on one lap, the car swerved, first toward the infield, then sharply back toward the wall. It hit head on, hard, and the well-liked driver was killed by the impact. Not knowing if the tires were at fault, the Hoosier Company pulled its product for the race. It turned out that it was a cut tire rather than any failure of the unit itself that caused the incident. As in 1988, Hoosier put up some stiff competition and helped a couple of struggling teams gain an edge, but succumbed to the safety concerns raised by any tire war and withdrew again.

There was something different about Marlin's No. 4 car at Daytona that year. You could hear it from the grandstands; the car had more of an Indy whine than the typical stock car grumble. Garage pundits predicted that some new adaptation would be found and disallowed, but the car passed all inspections and engine builder Runt Pittman and crew chief Tony Glover didn't have anything to say, so everyone waited for race day to see how it would play out.

It played out in Marlin's favor. He and Irvan were the class of the field for the 500, and with Irvan fighting an uncooperative set of tires, Marlin was able to take the lead and the win. It was his first victory in eighteen years of

LEFT: *Clifton "Coo Coo" Marlin joins his son Sterling in the winner's circle after the Kodak driver's 1995 Daytona 500 win. Both Marlins came up through the racing ranks out of the Nashville Speedway, where they were track champions (Coo Coo was crowned four times). Coo Coo ran Grand National and Winston Cup races through the 1960s and 1970s, but this was his first time in the series' victory lane.*

FOLLOWING PAGES: *The pack races three wide through the tri-oval in the 1996 Daytona 500. Dave Marcis (at left, in No. 71) never won the event but did have a record of his own going. Marcis ran more consecutive Daytona 500s than any other driver—thirty-two. Unfortunately his streak ended in 2000, when he failed to make the field.*

Winston Cup racing. Marlin's second win came at the same time in the same place the next year. Earnhardt fought his way through the field over the closing laps of the 1995 Daytona 500, but had nothing on the bright yellow Kodak Chevy. Dale had a more philosophical approach that year, remarking, "I don't reckon I'm *supposed* to win the damn thing!"

Marlin couldn't three-peat the race, though. In 1996 he placed second in his qualifier (behind Earnhardt), but a blown engine in the actual race sent him to the back of the finishing order. The race turned out to be a reprise of the "Dale and Dale Show," with the same contestants and, perhaps predictably, the same outcome. Dale Jarrett, now with an awesome Robert Yates team (No. 88), got his second Daytona 500 win, while Dale Earnhardt was once again the "first loser."

The 1997 Daytona 500: Hash Gordon

The Florida sun shone brightly for the thirty-ninth running of the season-opener. It was all the brighter for Darrell Waltrip's mirror-glossed No. 17 Chevy. Waltrip was celebrating his twenty-fifth year in the Winston Cup by running paint schemes through the year from all of his winning teams. For the Daytona 500, there was a special chrome finish that was a victory for the team's paint shop regardless of what else the car did that day.

As is so often the case at Daytona, the front row was a surprise. A Richard Childress car sat on the pole, but it wasn't the black No. 3. Mike Skinner was in his second year with the No. 31 team and had run a lap at a tick under 190 mph (305.7kph) to secure the front spot. On the outside was Steve Grissom, in his first year with Larry Hedrick and the No. 41 team.

Dale and Dale took their respective qualifying races. Earnhardt later had fun with the press saying, "Did you expect someone else?" Jeff Gordon, the 1995 champion and ten-time winner in 1996, started sixth. The 1997 Daytona truly signaled a changing of the guard. For the first time since 1973, there wasn't a Bud Moore No. 15 car in the Daytona 500 field. Larry Pearson, driver of Moore's unsponsored Ford, missed the cutoff in the qualifying race and wasn't able to make it on his time or on provisionals, so the veteran crew packed up and went home.

Earnhardt, Irvan, Mark Martin, Bill Elliott, and others exchanged the lead as the drafts sorted out through the opening laps. Gordon made his way to the top spot around lap fifty-seven and led for some time, but on lap 111, he cut down a tire and, narrowly averting a crash, limped down pit road. He managed to stay on the lead lap, but came out just in front of the snarling pack and would certainly be passed. To the DuPont team's relief, the caution flew only two laps later, and he was able to catch up to the end of the field.

Over the next seventy laps Earnhardt and Elliott did their best to pull away from Irvan and others so they could decide the race between them. Gordon was stuck in traffic and only slowly worked his way forward. With about twenty laps to go, though, he'd struggled up to third place, and when Earnhardt's No. 3 got a bit loose coming out of turn four, Gordon stuck his nose under the black Goodwrench car. The move took the air off Earnhardt's spoiler, and he wiggled, tagging the wall and then coming back across into Gordon. Gordon kept going, but Ernie Irvan and Dale Jarrett got wrapped up with Earnhardt, and No. 3 started tumbling down the front stretch. When the dust settled, the car was

BELOW: *Mike Skinner (in the Lowe's No. 31) and Steve Grissom (white car on left) lead the field to the start of the 1997 500. It was the first Winston Cup front-row start for either of those drivers. For the eventual winner, Jeff Gordon, the victory was the first leg of his Winston Million performance that year and put his team on the path to its second championship.*

RIGHT: *The Goodwrench crew works on the damaged No. 3 car after Dale Earnhardt's crash in the 1997 500. Although the considerable damage to the car had ended Earnhardt's chance for victory, the crew eventually got him back on track. Why didn't Dale have to visit the infield care center after the tumbling wreck? Such a trip is only mandatory is you cannot drive your car away from the accident, and Dale had made sure to drive the damaged vehicle to the pits.*

ABOVE: *Although Rick Hendrick's teams did well at the track in 1997, it was a tough year for the car owner. He battled a severe and debilitating illness at the same time his North Carolina Honda dealerships were under investigation for business improprieties. His drivers—Terry Labonte (left), Jeff Gordon (center), and Ricky Craven (right)— gave him something to smile about, though, as they swept the top three spots in that year's Daytona 500.*

back on its wheels but sorely battered. Earnhardt climbed out for the ambulance ride to the care center, but then seemed to notice something and walked back to the car. He asked the cleanup crew to try cranking it and, lo and behold, it started up. It wasn't as bad as he'd thought! He climbed back in and drove it to pit road for some quick repairs. The Goodwrench team cut off sheet metal, duct-taped to beat the band, and bungee-corded what was left. The Intimidator was laps down and the car looked like a junkyard special, but Dale made it back onto the track (to the exultation of his fans) and gamely finished the race.

That left sentimental favorite Bill Elliott in the lead with five laps to go, and the crowd holding its breath. When Bill looked in his mirror to see who was behind him, though, his heart must have skipped a beat. Jeff Gordon was lined up in second, and behind him were

Gordon's Hendrick Motorsports teammates Terry Labonte and Ricky Craven. Elliott was a sitting duck and knew it.

Gordon didn't wait long to make his move. Going into turn one on the restart, he dove low, way low—all the way down on the apron low— to challenge Elliott. As Elliott fought to hold off Gordon, the other Hendrick cars ganged up on him to the outside. Coming out onto the backstretch, it was No. 24 (Gordon), No. 5 (Labonte), and No. 25 (Craven)—then Bill Elliott. A multi-car crash brought out the caution flag as they crossed the line that lap, and set the finishing order as they cruised the last laps under yellow.

It made a great photo—the three teammates lined up together circling the track— and gave car owner Rick Hendrick, who was at home undergoing treatments for leukemia, something to smile about. Instead of the traditional driver-owner hug in victory lane, Gordon called Rick up on a cell phone, and the viewing audience heard Jeff's side of what was certainly a happy conversation.

In recent Daytona events, the entire field often runs three-wide, lap after lap. In this 1997 Daytona 500 photo, the pack is strung out after a restart. Quite a few of the drivers shown here had previously won the 500: Marlin (No. 4), Elliott (No. 94), Jarrett (No. 88) and Irvan (No. 28) accounted for seven of the previous twelve victories among them. The winners of the subsequent four races (Gordon, Earnhardt, and Jarrett) are in the photo as well.

The International Race of Champions (IROC)

WHAT RACE FAN HASN'T WONDERED who the best race car driver in the world is? Roger Penske and Les Richter conceived the International Race of Champions (IROC) in 1973 to answer just that question. Daytona International Speedway has been an important part of that series over most of its history.

IROC pits drivers from several different series against each other in identical cars. Theoretically, the only differences are the hands, eyes, and brains behind the wheel. In the first year of the races (1974), four drivers each from USAC, SCCA (Sports Car Club of America), NASCAR, and Formula One were invited to drive Porsche RSRs in four races: three at Riverside California and one on the road course at Daytona. SCCA champ Mark Donohue dominated the events, winning three of the four and the first IROC championship. In 1976, the Daytona race shifted to the big oval track, and NASCAR drivers had a more familiar venue where they could shine.

In 1979, the series moved to Michigan, Riverside, and Atlanta raceways, and Bobby Allison became the first stock car racer to win the IROC title. The series was discontinued in 1980 due to lack of sponsorship but picked back up in 1984 and returned to Daytona in 1985. Since then, the majority of races have been on oval tracks, and the style of cars used has shifted to American production models: the Dodge Daytona (a later version, not the wingback), the Chevy Camaro IROC-Z, and currently, the Pontiac Firebird TransAm. NASCAR drivers have dominated the series in the intervening years, with Dale Earnhardt and Mark Martin sharing the most titles at four apiece, although Al Unser Jr. still holds the record for most individual wins, with eleven victories. He'll likely remain unchallenged for some time—the next closest competitor was Dale Earnhardt (ten wins).

Earnhardt has the most IROC wins at Daytona (five), demonstrating that his legendary ability to "see the air" at the big track was not limited to just Winston Cup races. He was on his way to a sixth win in the series opener in 2001 until he was caught up in a crash on lap twenty-six when Jeff Burton suddenly cut across in front of him. Dale's car started the race bright green, but after the crew duct-taped down the torn sheet

metal, it was an abstract of green, blue, red, and silver. Despite the damage, he was back fighting for the lead in no time. As they came down to the last few laps, Eddie Cheever Jr. drafted up alongside him, then blocked Earnhardt by cutting left. He took the Intimidator all the way into the grass and Earnhardt slid across the infield. In an incredible show of skill, he held the car in and made it back on track, though far out of contention. Cheever lost his momentum as well, and NASCAR drivers Dale Jarrett and Ricky Rudd were left to fight it out for the lead. Jarrett wasn't shy about wanting to win his first IROC event and rubbed fenders with Rudd to eke out a two-foot (.6m) advantage at the line.

OPPOSITE: *The first IROC series race at Daytona, in 1974. That was the only year the field ran a non-American make of car (Porsche). The specific car a driver runs in each race (and thus his number and car color) is determined by lottery to try and keep the field as even, and the outcome as strictly based on driver ability, as possible.*

ABOVE: *In 1975 the IROC series switched to Chevy Camaros. Al Unser (shown at left) began his winning tradition in the series with the Daytona race shown here.*

LEFT: *Dale Earnhardt holds the trophy for the 2000 Daytona IROC win as he shakes hands with track owner Bill France Jr. This was the last of Earnhardt's remarkable eleven IROC wins and put him on the path to his fourth IROC championship, which he won that year.*

Chapter Five

DALE EARNHARDT AT DAYTONA

DALE EARNHARDT HOLDS QUITE A FEW RECORDS at Daytona International Speedway. Up through 1998, he'd won seven Busch Grand National races there, more than any other driver. He'd won the Busch Clash (later Bud Shootout) six times; just about every 125-mile (201.1km) qualifier he'd run, including the last nine in a row; and twice, the July 400-mile (643.7km) race. And then there's the record he probably would have liked someone else to assume: most consecutive losses in the 500.

Fireball Roberts suffered through several years of abject failure before even finishing a Daytona 500. It took Darrell Waltrip seventeen years and Buddy Baker nineteen to break through to the winner's circle. Earnhardt was one up on Buddy and going into his twentieth running. Why was Earnhardt's streak such a big deal? After all, there have been plenty of good drivers who've never won at Daytona.

ABOVE: *Earnhardt focuses on the task at hand, putting on his gear as he prepares to qualify for the 2001 Daytona 500. When Earnhardt went through a winless spell in 1997, his detractors speculated that his escalating business ventures were distracting him from racing. His 1998 Daytona win and subsequent victories at other tracks made it clear that he still had the drive and ability to win races.*

LEFT: *The No. 3 car often hosted special "guest sponsors" for distinctive events (e.g., The Winston, the Busch Clash, and so on). The Warner Brothers Tasmanian devil character known as Taz (depicted on the hood of the car) was featured in Chevy's television ads for the Monte Carlo and seemed a good match for the super-aggressive racer known as the Intimidator.*

When the No. 3 team arrived at the big track in 1998, it wasn't just the Daytona curse they were battling. They had another streak going at the start of that season also: a fifty-nine-race winless streak. The team posted two wins in 1996, but the last of those was back in March. Championship-winning crew chief Andy Petree left Childress Racing at the end of that season to take over the Skoal No. 33 team, and the adjustment to new crew chief Larry McReynolds had not gone well. The team was winless through 1997, the first such season for Earnhardt since 1981. A Daytona 500 win in 1998 would heal a lot of wounds for the Goodwrench team, and they were geared up to give their best, plus some, once again. Against nineteen years of history, the odds makers picked Earnhardt as a favorite for the race.

The 1998 Daytona 500: Vindicated!

NASCAR celebrated its fiftieth birthday in 1998, and its golden anniversary was marked by a drastic renovation in the Winston Million program. The previous year Jeff Gordon had become the second, and last, driver to win the prize. For 1998, R.J. Reynolds decided to sweeten the pot.

The new program was called the "No Bull 5" and it was a dandy. Five special races were selected (the Brickyard 400 at Indianapolis was added to the four Winston Million events). If any of the top five finishers in one of those races won the next selected event, they got $1,000,000. On top of that, five fans were selected and assigned to the eligible drivers. If the driver won, the

ABOVE: **NASCAR kicked off its fiftieth year at Daytona International Speedway in 1998. Rick Hendrick made the most of the golden anniversary by renumbering his No. 25 car, driven by Ricky Craven, to No. 50 for the season.**

OPPOSITE: *Dale Earnhardt leads the pack in the closing laps of the 1998 Daytona 500, his teammate Mike Skinner right behind him. The two were really teammates only off the track, and were more competitive than coopera- tive with each other during a race. As only one car stood between him and a first win, Skinner was probably more determined than ever to get by, regardless of the garage the lead car came from.*

In Earnhardt's case, the February classic stood out because it was an exception, the only missing achievement on his otherwise amazing resume. Seven championships had tied him with the guy everyone calls "The King." His seventy trophies (just counting points races) had put him sixth on the all-time NASCAR win list. He'd won on short tracks and superspeedways and even notched a long-sought-after road-course win. Worst of all was that, year after year, he had been so good at Daytona. He'd qualify well, win the 125-qualifier, plus other assorted lead-in races, and run like the wind through most of the Sunday race. Then something would go wrong.

Through the first half of the 1980s, he suffered recurring engine problems. In 1986, he ran out of gas while leading near the end. In 1989, he lost when Waltrip *didn't* run out of gas. In 1990, he cut a tire while leading past the white flag. Crashes and last-lap passes by that other Dale (Jarrett) took care of most of the 1990s. It looked as though nature itself was against him when one year an errant sea gull got caught in the slipstream of the draft and flew right into Earnhardt's front grille.

assigned fan got a million of his or her own. It was a big boost in dollars and added quite a bit of extra excitement through the year to each of the five races.

Bobby Labonte had joined Joe Gibbs' Interstate Batteries No. 18 team in 1995 and had become quite a strong performer on super-speedways. He ran the pole-setting lap for the Daytona race (the tenth pole of his career) at a convincing 192.415 mph (309.662kph). His brother Terry (the 1984 and 1996 Winston Cup champ) ran the second fastest, so it was an all-Labonte front row. Adding to the excitement, if any of the top five finishers from the Winston 500 the previous year—either of the Labonte Brothers, Ken Schrader, John Andretti, or Ernie Irvan—won the Daytona 500, he would also win the $1 million under the No Bull 5 program.

Sterling Marlin, now with the No. 40 team of Felix Sabates, showed that he hadn't forgotten

how to win at Daytona and took the first qualifier race. Sterling was another driver on a winless streak (since 1996), and the victory in the 125-miler was a welcome respite. Dale Earnhardt ran in the second qualifier. Right from the green flag, he made it clear that he was taking no prisoners at Daytona that year. His hands-down win broke the team's long drought, and put him fourth on the grid.

It was no surprise when the No. 3 car pushed to the front early in the 500 and stayed there. It was a typical Earnhardt-at-Daytona scenario: Dale had led more than half the race and was running up front near the end. Everyone in the crowd, and probably Dale himself, was wondering what would happen that year to derail the Goodwrench express.

At restrictor-plate tracks, it can help to have a teammate in the field, and Earnhardt hooked up with the other Childress car of Mike

RIGHT: *The Penske team cars of Rusty Wallace (No. 2) and Jeremy Mayfield (No. 12) ran together on the track through much of the 1998 season. Penske Racing seemed to adapt better than many Ford teams to the new Taurus model that year and enjoyed solid runs and a pair of wins. Here, the teammates hook up to make a charge on Earnhardt in the closing laps of the 1998 Daytona 500. Gordon (No. 24) was the spoiler, though, and none of these contestants could mount the charge needed to pass the black car.*

Skinner. They were 1-2 when a caution flag flew at lap 174. Earnhardt made it out of the pits first, taking just two tires, and led Skinner and Penske teammates Rusty Wallace and Jeremy Mayfield back to the green.

Skinner and Earnhardt tried to split away from the others, but the Penske Fords stayed in close touch. Jeff Gordon and Bobby Labonte (a No Bull 5 contender) also hooked up with the lead cars and turned it into a six-way battle.

With a handful of circuits left, the Penske duo broke out to pass Skinner, but then were split up by a charging Jeff Gordon. Earnhardt had to be smiling as he watched the battle of the cars behind him. With two laps to go, Dale faced a new challenger. Bobby Labonte had been quiet through most of the race but was making a strong onslaught in the waning laps

and had driven around the others to pull up directly behind No. 3.

On lap 199, a trio of cars spun along the backstretch and the yellow flag flew. Whoever made it back to the flag first would likely win the race (assuming the last lap would be under caution, with no passing allowed). All Earnhardt had to do was hold on for one more. A hush fell as everyone waited for lightning to strike the black car; he'd been this close before and it had always gone wrong.

Labonte and Mayfield made spirited charges at Earnhardt (Labonte had a million dollars on the line, after all), but the streak had run its course. Dale used a lapped car to block the challengers, took the yellow flag, made it around the caution lap, and won the Daytona 500. Everybody, whether you liked Earnhardt or

ABOVE: *Dale Earnhardt crosses the line in 1998 for his first and only Daytona 500 win. This photo is one of the most popular ever among NASCAR fans, and with good reason: a multitude of Earnhardt fans support a multimillion-dollar industry in Intimidator-related souvenir sales. Just about anything with Dale's picture, or a picture of his car, on it sells like hotcakes.*

ABOVE: *Dale Earnhardt does doughnuts in the Daytona tri-oval infield in celebration of his 1998 500 win. The 2001 season saw a competition of sorts arise among race winners to see who could execute the most perfect postrace doughnuts and burnout. Track management often frowns on this type of activity because of the damage it does to the turf (not to mention the grass paintings), but no one was inclined to argue with Earnhardt over this one.*

RIGHT: *In a fitting show of respect in an ultra-competitive sport, the crews of the other teams lined up to offer Earnhardt congratulations on his long-awaited Daytona 500 win in 1998.*

not, was a bit misty-eyed as No. 3 spun dough-nuts in the infield in front of the flag stand. In an unprecedented and unanimous show of respect, crewmembers from every team lined up to slap palms with the victorious racer as he drove slowly along pit road to the winner's circle.

For the first time after a Daytona 500, it was a relaxed and smiling Dale Earnhardt that the press got to interview. At the postrace conference, he had a stuffed animal to offer up to some other driver. As he put it, "This monkey's finally off *my* back!"

Heading into the New Millennium

The 1998 Daytona win set Dale Earnhardt up as a candidate for the $1 million bonus at the next No Bull 5 race. Earnhardt didn't manage the follow-up win, but Dale Jarrett did later in the year, as did Jeff Gordon—twice, in the World 600 and Southern 500. All told, R.J. Reynolds paid out $6 million for the program in its first season.

Prior to the 1999 Daytona race, the press seemed a bit out of stride. After all, they didn't have that old familiar story to rely on: "Will Earnhardt finally win at Daytona?" In a burst of creativity, they came up with "Will Earnhardt win his second Daytona 500?"

LEFT: *Victory lane celebrations after the 1998 Daytona 500. The win was Earnhardt's seventy-first as a driver and Richard Childress' sixty-fourth as a car owner.*

BELOW: *Victory lane at Daytona in 1998. A year or so later, NASCAR outlawed the postrace dance on the car's roof. In some postrace inspections, several winners had been found to have rooflines below the regulated height (which would confer an advantage on the track), ostensibly due to the drivers having jumped all over them after a win. Such behavior now automatically incurs at least a stiff fine. The winning driver in the next race you watch might stand on the window frame, but no higher.*

Earnhardt gave every indication he could conquer Daytona again by winning his tenth straight qualifier race. Bobby Labonte got his first Daytona trophy in the other 125-miler. Those two lined up behind 1998 Winston Cup champ Jeff Gordon, whose 195.067 mph (313.93kph) lap put him squarely on the pole. A second Joe Gibbs team, in its rookie year, snagged the outside pole. Former Indy Racing League champ Tony Stewart had moved over to stock cars the previous year and then graduated from Busch Grand National rookie to Gibbs' No. 20 Winston Cup team (with Home Depot as sponsor) in 1999. The team had high hopes for the rookie, and the front-row-qualifying run started him off on the right foot.

Jeff Gordon, Mike Skinner, and Bobby Labonte swapped the lead through the first fifty laps of the main event. Rusty Wallace, who'd never had much luck in restrictor plate races, was making a strong showing and took over at the point from lap 58 through 121, then again,

starting on lap 153. With about twenty-five laps to go, Bobby Hamilton went into a spin, bringing out a caution. The teams suddenly faced a decision about pit stops. The Penske teams of Rusty Wallace and Jeremy Mayfield thought both drivers had the gas and tires to go all the way. The two were about the only cars that stayed on the track, and as all of the other teams lined up behind them with four fresh tires, it looked like it might not have been the best call.

Wallace and Mayfield held off the challengers on the restart—at least until Earnhardt and Gordon had worked their way back through the field. They passed Mayfield and lined up behind Rusty, who was by then struggling to stay in front on the old tires. Gordon pulled up alongside Earnhardt to challenge for second, and Wallace was hoping for a prolonged battle back there. Gordon made the pass quickly, though, and pulled up on the leader's bumper.

As they came up on a slower car, Gordon dove into the narrowing gap and pulled off a daring pass. Earnhardt and Mike Skinner had freight-trained Wallace as well, and No. 3 was in position to go for the repeat win. With restrictor plates, though, out front is usually the best place to be, and Gordon kept the Intimidator in his rearview mirror to win his second Daytona 500.

Rookie Tony Stewart slid back to a twenty-eighth-place finish but more than made up for

FOLLOWING PAGES: *Winning in NASCAR's elite series is absolutely a team effort. The driver and crew chief are the focus of reporters and fans, but every member of the crew can critically affect the outcome of a race. Here, the No. 88 team moves the car through the garage area in the days leading up to the successful 2000 Daytona 500 run.*

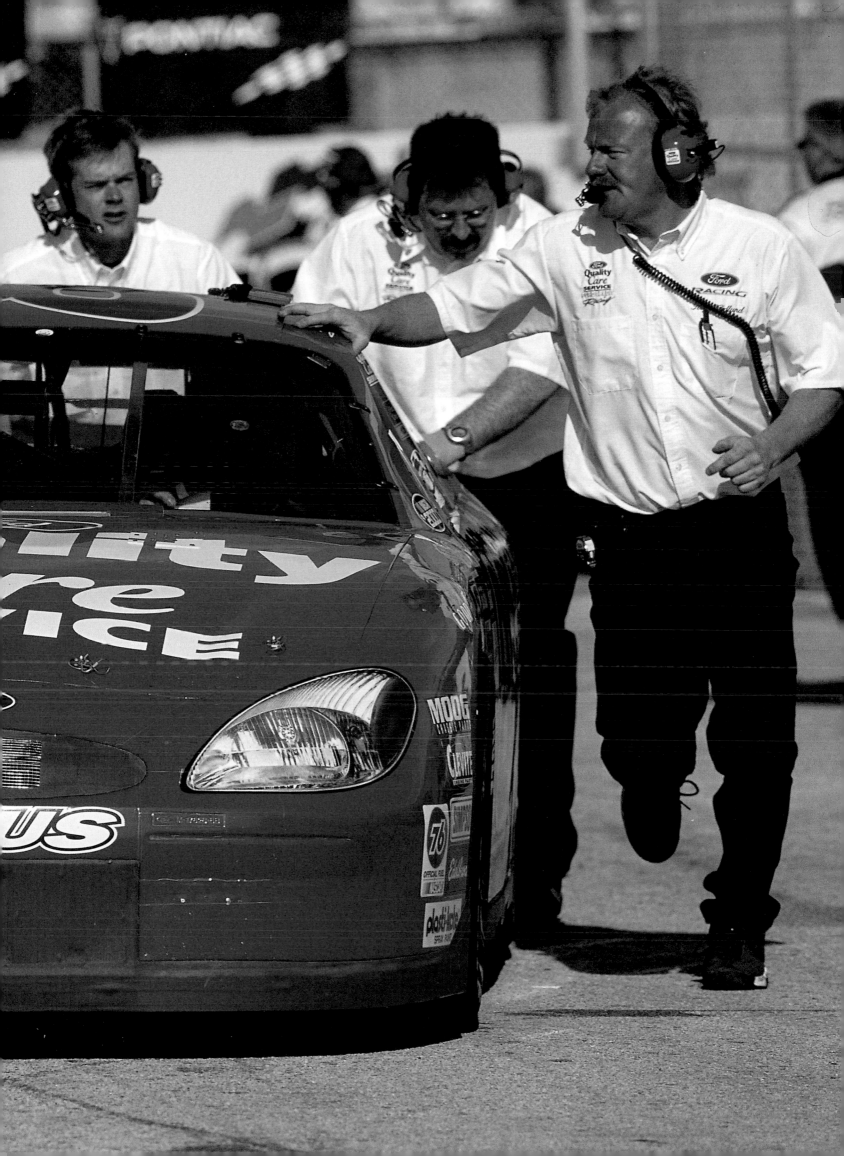

RIGHT: *On his way to his third Daytona 500 victory, in 2000, Dale Jarrett pits for the final time during the race. The times for pit stops have been dropping over the last few years, and nowadays it's not unusual for a top team to finish a four-tire stop in fewer than 15 seconds. For perspective, pit times in the 1960s for the same activity were in the 25-to-30-second range.*

BELOW: *The field streams by the start/finish line at the beginning of the 2000 Daytona 500. Sure to be immortalized in trivia contests henceforth, Dale Jarrett was the winner of the first NASCAR points race of the new millennium.*

OPPOSITE: *The pressures of owning his own team began to weigh on Ricky Rudd by the end of the twentieth century. Single-car teams are at a distinct disadvantage nowadays and Rudd's fortunes slipped from the 1998 through 2000 seasons. When his primary sponsor, Tide, announced they would leave him at the end of the 2000 season, Rudd gave up the ghost and took the open No. 28 ride at Robert Yates Racing. With Rudd behind the wheel, the team notched its first win since 1997 in 2001 at Pocono. Here, Yates teammates Rudd (left) and Dale Jarrett share thoughts before a race.*

it with a record three wins over the course of his first season.

In 2000, along with a new millennium, came a new hand at NASCAR's helm. Bill France Jr. had named Mike Helton to succeed him as president of the organization. France would remain as chairman, but it would be Helton steering the ship day-to-day.

Speed Weeks started out with a bit of deja vu as Bill Elliott scored his first win since 1994 in the first qualifier. More surprising was that Dale Earnhardt was in that race. Ricky Rudd had called it quits on his independently owned team after 1999 and moved to the Robert Yates No. 28 organization, replacing Kenny Irwin. Irwin was in the No. 42 car and had high hopes for the year. Those hopes were cut short, however, when a crash during a practice lap at New Hampshire International Speedway in July claimed his life. The crash occurred at the same spot where, just months before, fourth-generation driver

Adam Petty (Kyle Petty's son) had been killed in a similar crash in his Busch Grand National car.

Dale Jarrett looked like the car to beat on Sunday, despite damage to No. 88 in a crash during "Happy Hour" practice (the last session before the race) the previous day. When the green flag dropped, he cleared up any doubt, moving past leader Mike Skinner on lap five and pulling away.

With about fifty laps to go, it looked like there might be another first-time winner visiting Daytona's victory lane. Johnny Benson, in the MB2 Motorsports No. 10 car, with a pickup sponsor for the one race, worked up into the lead and, surprisingly, held onto it. Only six laps remained, and Benson was still in control. Then a crash brought out the caution flag. Dale Jarrett, running in second, had the better car on restarts and when the green flew again on lap 197, he was able to dart around Benson and win his third Daytona.

RIGHT: *The 2000 Daytona 500 was perhaps the least interesting in recent memory. Dale Jarrett—who probably enjoyed it immensely—had an easy time with the field, leading most of the race and fending off all comers with ease. There were only nine lead changes, a record low, which focused attention once more on the drawbacks of restrictor plates. Rules changes were enacted for the 2001 event to put a bit more of the outcome in the drivers' hands, and to enliven the show for new broadcast partners NBC/FOX.*

LEFT: *The No. 88 crew cele-brates their win in the 2000 Daytona 500. Much has been made of second-generation drivers, but such winning legacies are carried forth among crews as well. The No. 88 chief is Todd Parrott, son of championship-winning chief mechanic Buddy Parrott.*

BELOW: *The last twenty laps were probably the most exciting of the 2000 Daytona 500. The dominant car, the No. 88, ended up fifth in line on a restart when other teams went with a quicker two-tire stop under caution and got back on track ahead of Dale Jarrett. Jarrett moved up to second, but needed another restart to help him get by leader Johnny Benson. The race's final caution came out with only two laps to go and the last laps were run under the yellow flag (shown here).*

The 2001 Daytona 500: Triumph and Tragedy

NASCAR's fifty-third season promised to be a pivotal one for the sport. NASCAR had announced new television deals with FOX and NBC the previous year, and fans were skeptical that those upstarts in motorsports coverage could match the quality and dedication of ESPN, ABC, TNN, et al. There would be a couple of old hands behind the mikes, but the new color commentary team would be Darrell Waltrip (who'd retired after 2000, his twenty-eighth season) and former crew chiefs Larry McReynolds and Jeff Hammond. D.W. was expected to be a treat and wasted no time bringing his unique outlook to the proceedings when he said, "Victory circle is like heaven—they open the gates and you drive on in."

The year 2001 was also the first time since 1978 that a Dodge car would run in NASCAR's premier series. Chrysler-Daimler had announced in 1999 that it would field the Dodge Intrepid starting in 2001, and named former Jeff Gordon crew chief Ray Evernham as its lead man. Evernham formed two teams of his own (with fan favorite Bill Elliott back in No. 9 and rookie Casey Atwood) and helped entice several other prominent teams to Mopar. Among them was an old Chrysler stalwart, Petty Enterprises. Petty would run three Dodges in 2001 (No. 43, No. 44 with Buckshot Jones driving, and Kyle in what had originally been his son's No. 45). Bill Davis, Chip Ganassi (the CART series owner took over Felix Sabates' operation), and the Melling team went with the Intrepids as well.

Yet another new aspect of the 2001 season was a modified set of rules for the restrictor plate tracks. FOX network executives were undoubtedly concerned that a yawner like the previous year's Daytona (with only nine lead changes) might kill their fledgling investment right off. To address that, and to try to put more control of the car back in the drivers' hands, NASCAR changed the bodies and carburetor plates for 2001. The openings in the

plates were larger, allowing more air in, and thus more horsepower at the gas pedal. To cut the speed, they changed the body templates, upsizing the spoilers, adding roof rails, and raising the front air dam half an inch (1.3cm). The effect was supposed to give drivers more optional power and handling but still keep the speed down. At Daytona, small changes can have big effects, and many drivers elected to hold their comments on the changes until after the race.

Elliott immediately showed what the new Dodges could do. He put the old familiar No. 9 on the pole at Daytona once again with a lap at 183.57 mph (295.42kph). At least one part of NASCAR's new rules program worked—speeds were down by about 12 mph (19.3kph). A surprise on the outside pole was Stacy Compton, in the Melling No. 92 Dodge.

ABOVE: *Dale Earnhardt (right) and Kyle Petty (left) talk in the garage before the Daytona 500 in 2001. Earnhardt was aggressive on the track and could be a hard man in general, but his friends and acquaintances spoke glowingly of him as a thoughtful and considerate individual.*

OPPOSITE: *Kyle Petty suffered the terrible pain of losing a loved one to the sport. Kyle's son, Adam, was slated to move up to Winston Cup in the No. 45 car in 2001 as the fourth generation of Petty to race in the series. Tragically, Adam lost his life in a Busch Grand National series crash at the track in Loudon, New Hampshire.*

Earnhardt put on his usual performance in the first of the 125-mile (200km) races also, but was cashiered at the end by Sterling Marlin. Marlin seemed to have the best Dodge under race conditions. Elliott turned in only mediocre finishes in both the Shootout and his qualifier; the new team had the right talent but also clearly had some more homework to do. Dale Earnhardt Jr., who'd shown his potential with a couple of wins in 2000, his rookie year, battled neck and neck with Mike Skinner at the end of the second qualifier. Skinner edged him out by a bumper to earn the fourth starting spot in the 500.

The phrase most often used by the teams to describe now the cars were handling in the lead-up events was "pushy loose." Teams were having some trouble adjusting to the new setups and getting the cars to turn freely. As a result, the drivers would oversteer them in the turns, to the point where the back ends "broke loose" (hence the phrase "pushy loose"). The FOX broadcast had some clever graphics to illustrate the racing concepts, clearly hoping they'd attracted a broader audience than the usual fans. However, they did make one serious gaffe in the qualifiers and Shootout shows: erasing the sponsors on the car illustrations they used to segue in and out of the coverage. Only a few sponsors were shown, apparently ones that had some special arrangement with the network. You just don't mess with race sponsors, and that message came across loudly and quickly. By Sunday, every little picture had the appropriate corporate logo accurately depicted.

As soon as Super Bowl–winning quarterback Terry Bradshaw waved the green flag for the Daytona 500, it looked like Elliott may have been playing possum through the other races. He and Dodge teammate Stacy Compton took off with a big jump on the field. It didn't last long, though, and Marlin took over the lead after just a lap. "Little E," as Earnhardt Jr. is known, grabbed the point briefly, then Marlin moved back up. Winston Cup rookie (but Craftsman Truck series champ) Ron Hornaday, in A.J. Foyt's No. 14 car, rock-

The first opportunity to see how fast the Dodges would race in the pack came with the Bud Shootout. The Shootout is a non-points event that is reserved for pole winners from the previous year. The field was expanded in 2001 to include past winners of the event as well, and that is how Elliott made it in. With that change, it was a bigger starting field than usual: eighteen cars lined up. Bobby Labonte and Dale Earnhardt (a six-time winner of the race) broke away early, but were chased down by Dale Jarrett's No. 88 (with new sponsorship from United Parcel Service). It came down to Earnhardt and Tony Stewart at the end, though, with Stewart making a bold three-wide pass down the backstretch to snatch win number seven from Earnhardt and get his first Daytona trophy.

eted through the field, moving from thirty-ninth to second in just five laps. Hornaday stayed near the front until he was penalized for speeding on pit road.

Dodges dominated the first half of the event, with Marlin and Ward Burton (in Bill Davis' No. 22 Dodge) as the fastest cars. It was an exciting and ever-changing race, though. The previous year, fans watched a single file of cars snake around the track lap after lap, with only nine changes for the lead during the entire event. Well, it worked: the Bud Shootout even had nineteen lead changes. The new rule seemed to open up the field a bit more and allow drivers to make more passes on their own or with limited help. The three-wide freight trains were still there, but the draft was no longer the only way to move up.

Burton led the most laps in the race and was perhaps the car to beat, if only he could be around at the end. A big crash on lap 175

ended the day for quite a few potential winners, though. Robby (no relation to Jeff) Gordon, in the No. 4 Kodak Chevy, touched the back of Ward Burton, who then spun into Tony Stewart. Stewart's No. 20 turned and lifted up over the top of Burton's car. Behind them carnage ensued, as tightly packed cars swerved and braked to try to miss the airborne Home Depot Pontiac but were then piled into from behind. Stewart tumbled a dozen times, end over end, from one side of the track to the other, a good fifteen feet (4.6m) off the ground at some points. Once the smoke cleared, eighteen cars were sitting still or limping around to pit road. Among them were top contenders Burton, Jeff Gordon, Bobby Labonte, and Mark Martin. Amazingly, there were no serious injuries, though Stewart was taken to the local hospital for observation.

"The Big One" changed the complexion of the race altogether. When the green flag flew again, it was an Earnhardt fan's vision of paradise.

BELOW: *Dale Earnhardt Jr. poses with his car on pit road during Speed Weeks, 2001. His life would soon be drastically altered by the fatal crash of his father's car in that year's 500. In the wake of his father's death, "Little E" has become a favorite of many of the dyed-in-the-wool Earnhardt fans. The young man shows the same determination and desire to win as his father and clearly learned his racing lessons from the master. But he already displays the patience and on-track smarts that took Dale Sr. a number of years to develop.*

Michael Waltrip, in his first race with a new Dale Earnhardt, Inc. (DEI) team, was in the lead in No. 15. Behind him was another DEI car with Dale Jr. And behind Dale Jr. was the old man himself. Both Sterling Marlin and Rusty Wallace had fallen back with trouble earlier in the race but were able to move back up to contend with the leaders through the last twenty laps.

In 1993, Ned Jarrett was in the broadcast booth to coach his son to an emotional victory at Daytona. This time it was brother Darrell Waltrip who was doing everything but pushing the gas pedal to keep "Mikey" in the lead. The younger Waltrip was winless after more than 450 Winston Cup races—what a boost a Daytona victory would be to his career. Through the last laps it appeared to be just a matter of time until Earnhardt Sr. would put the moves on his "employees" and take the lead.

But lap after lap, Waltrip drove the right line and neither father nor son was able to get past.

"One to go buddy—keep it low, keep it low," advised the elder Waltrip as Michael took the white flag. "Make that back straightaway wide." Down the backstretch, Sterling Marlin challenged Earnhardt for third as they came up on the slower car of Ken Schrader. That battle clogged up traffic behind, allowing Waltrip and Earnhardt Jr. to pull away to a ten-car-length lead. Through turn four, Waltrip was edging ahead. "You got it, you got it!" screamed the jubilant older brother as Michael Waltrip streaked under the checkered flag for his first Winston Cup win!

As Waltrip and Earnhardt Jr. headed for the finish line, Mike Joy hollered, "Oh, big trouble, big wreck behind them." Marlin and Earnhardt Sr. had been running side by side when Marlin just tagged the left rear of the No.

3 car. Earnhardt Sr. swerved toward the infield, caught it, then broke loose to the outside. He collided hard head-on with the turn-four wall. Ken Schrader was trapped up high and had nowhere to go but into the right side of the black car. Rusty Wallace slid by Marlin to take third place as No. 3 and No. 36 slid down to the infield.

Waltrip and the No. 15 team celebrated in victory lane, waiting for their car owner to turn up to offer his support. It wasn't until later that they learned that Dale Earnhardt was being cut out of the No. 3 car by emergency crews and rushed to the hospital. It didn't look like that bad of a crash, but something had gone wrong. The crowd waited in sick anticipation as NASCAR officials shrouded the wrecked No. 3 after the ambulance left.

It was about an hour later that the announcement came. Dale Earnhardt, seven-time Winston Cup champion and arguably the best stock car racer of all time, had been killed in the crash. The racing world was stunned. What had been perhaps the most exciting

Daytona 500 race since 1959 had become a day of tragedy and sorrow.

Coverage of the crash was intense. It was doubly tragic that it took the death of the sport's biggest hero to achieve the front-page coverage in national newspapers and magazines that NASCAR had sought for so long. NASCAR teams and fans pulled together in their mourning for the fallen champion, and the remainder of the 2001 season would be marked by commemorations and remembrances.

Earnhardt's death was a cruel blow to the sport he loved, not only due to his absence but also in the repercussions it brought to NASCAR. It was later announced that the severe injuries leading to his death were likely caused by a separation of his seat belt on impact. Unanswered questions about the nature and cause of the injuries remain, however, and NASCAR's close-lipped approach to resolution has led to questions about the organization's commitment to driver safety and methods of conducting business.

OPPOSITE TOP: *NASCAR's recent report on Earnhardt's crash suggests that the effects of the No. 36 car's collision into the side of the No. 3 just before the latter's head-on impact into the wall may have played a large role in the unfortunate outcome. The combination of lateral and forward forces (and the manner in which the No. 3 car's belts were installed in the cockpit) could have twisted Earnhardt's harness in a way that caused it to separate.*

BELOW: *On February 18, 2001, not long after winning the Great American Race, Michael Waltrip had one of the most thrilling experiences of his life when he was presented with the Daytona 500 trophy. Standing here in victory lane next to his wife, Buffy, Michael did not yet know that Dale Earnhardt—his employer and one of the greatest stock car drivers of all time—had just died on the track.*

RIGHT: *A sea of RVs at Daytona. Camping in the infield is a way for families to enjoy Speed Weeks without the hassle of traffic and hotels. Some fans feel the need to express their team allegiance with more than a baseball cap or T-shirt, and full-size flags and pennants adorn many of the vehicles*

OPPOSITE: *The sun sets behind the grandstands at Daytona. The work goes on long after the race is over for many, including track and grounds maintenance personnel, NASCAR scorekeepers and officials, and the crews that have to prepare for the race at Rockingham just days away.*

The Future

As we begin the race through the twenty-first century, perhaps the only thing about the future of NASCAR that we can predict with any certainty is that things will change—the cars, the teams, and the tracks themselves. There will be change at Daytona as well, as evidenced by the rules modifications that were made to improve the quality of competition at the restrictor plate tracks. And it takes no great skill at fortune-telling to see that the "Birthplace of Speed" will continue to play a pivotal role in the series that engendered it.

Daytona continues to be the bellwether of the sport. As the first stop on the circuit, it's the place each year where the winter's rumors are confirmed or dismissed. Fast talk translates to lap speeds, and the inevitable changes are tested against the hard reality of the racetrack.

It's a track where heroes are made, and all too often, lost. With the passing of Dale Earnhardt, it is impossible not to wonder who will be the next driver to wage such a long and epic struggle against the famous track.

The Winston Cup series has certainly grown far beyond reliance on any one race for its success, but it is still important to have a focus, an icon that identifies the sport. When the IRL and Indy car series split, CART lost the race that signifies top-quality open-wheel racing to most fans: the Indianapolis 500. That loss hurt the series immeasurably. Winston Cup fans all have their own favorite tracks, but Daytona is the symbol of NASCAR.

There are lots of trophies for Cup drivers throughout a season, but the most coveted is, and will remain, the one awarded at the end of the Daytona 500, the Great American Race!

FOLLOWING PAGES: *The show is over, and for the first time in many days it's truly quiet at Daytona International Speedway. As teams head north to their home bases in North Carolina and Virginia, drivers, owners, and crewmembers contemplate their Daytona experience. For some, dreams were fulfilled; for many others, those dreams evaporated with a crunch of sheet metal or the acrid tang of burned rubber. One thing all departing competitors have in common is the desire to come back and try again, next year.*

Bibliography

Books

Falk, Duane. *The Winston Cup.* New York: MetroBooks, 2000.

Fielden, Greg. *Forty Years of Stock Car Racing,* vols. 1–4. Surfside Beach, SC: Galfield Press, 1992, 1992, 1990, 1989.

———. *Forty Years of Stock Car Racing Plus Four.* Surfside Beach, SC: Galfield Press, 1994.

Golenbock, Peter, and Greg Fielden. *The Stock Car Racing Encyclopedia.* New York: Macmillan, 1997.

Higgins, Tom. *NASCAR Greatest Races.* New York: Tehabi Books, 1999.

———, and Steve Waid. *Brave in Life: Junior Johnson.* Phoenix, AZ: David Bull Publishing, 1999.

Houston, Rick. *Second to None.* Phoenix, AZ: David Bull Publishing, 2001.

Hunter, Don, and Al Pearce. *The Illustrated History of Stock Car Racing.* Osceola, WI: MBI Publishing, 1998.

———, and Ben White. *American Stock Car Racers.* Osceola, WI: Motorbooks International, 1997.

Latford, Bob. *Built for Speed.* Philadelphia, PA: Courage Books, 1999.

Moriarty, Frank. *The Encyclopedia of Stock Car Racing.* New York: Friedman/Fairfax Publishers, 1998.

Various. *NASCAR The Thunder of America.* Del Mar, CA: Tehabi Books, 1998.

Various. *NASCAR Winston Cup Yearbooks: 1973-2001.* Charlotte, NC: UMI Publications, 1973–2001.

Riggs, D. Randy. *Flat-Out Racing.* New York: Friedman/Fairfax Publishers, 1995.

Various. *American Racing Classics.* Charlotte, NC: Street & Smith's Sports Group, 2000.

Vehorn, Frank. *The Intimidator.* Asheboro, NC: Down Home Press, 1991.

Zeller, Bob. *Mark Martin: Driven to Race.* Phoenix, AZ: David Bull Publishing, 1997.

Periodicals

Various. *The Official NASCAR Preview and Press Guide,* 1991–2001. Charlotte, NC: UMI Publications, 1991–2001.

Websites

Bonneville Salt Flats: www.lib.utah.edu/spc/photo/bonn/bonn.htm

Daytona 500: www.daytona500.com

Daytona Beach & Road Memories: www.speedzone70.tripod.com/beach-road.html

Daytona International Speedway: www.daytonaintlspeedway.com

Daytona USA: www.daytonausa.com

International Motorsports Hall of Fame: www.motorsportshalloffame.com

International Speedway Corporations: www.iscmotorsports.com

Jayski's NASCAR Silly Season Site: www.jayski.com

Living Legends of Auto Racing: www.lloar.com

NASCAR Online: www.nascar.com

Rolex 24 Hours: www.rolex24.com

Speed Fx (50 Years of NASCAR History): www.speedfx.com/history/history_index.shtml

That's Racin': www.thatsracin.com

Truevalue IROC Racing Series: www.iroc-racing.com/current_season/frontpage.html

NASCAR Grand National/Winston Cup Champions

1949	Red Byron	1958	Lee Petty	1967	Richard Petty	1976	Cale Yarborough	1985	Darrell Waltrip	1994	Dale Earnhardt
1950	Bill Rexford	1959	Lee Petty	1968	David Pearson	1977	Cale Yarborough	1986	Dale Earnhardt	1995	Jeff Gordon
1951	Herb Thomas	1960	Rex White	1969	David Pearson	1978	Cale Yarborough	1987	Dale Earnhardt	1996	Terry Labonte
1952	Tim Flock	1961	Ned Jarrett	1970	Bobby Isaac	1979	Richard Petty	1988	Bill Elliott	1997	Jeff Gordon
1953	Herb Thomas	1962	Joe Weatherly	1971	Richard Petty	1980	Dale Earnhardt	1989	Rusty Wallace	1998	Jeff Gordon
1954	Lee Petty	1963	Joe Weatherly	1972	Richard Petty	1981	Darrell Waltrip	1990	Dale Earnhardt	1999	Dale Jarrett
1955	Tim Flock	1964	Richard Petty	1973	Benny Parsons	1982	Darrell Waltrip	1991	Dale Earnhardt	2000	Bobby Labonte
1956	Buck Baker	1965	Ned Jarrett	1974	Richard Petty	1983	Bobby Allison	1992	Alan Kulwicki	2001	Jeff Gordon
1957	Buck Baker	1966	David Pearson	1975	Richard Petty	1984	Terry Labonte	1993	Dale Earnhardt		

Daytona International Superspeedway Records

	Winston Cup Daytona 500	Pepsi 400	Busch Grand National NAPA Auto Parts 300	True Value IROC	ARCA Discount Auto 2000	Rolex 24 HRS
Most Starts	Richard Petty, 32	Richard Petty, 32	Red Farmer, 21	Al Unser Jr., 12	Bob Dotter, 18	Hurley Haywood, 26
Pole Speed, mph (kph)	210.364 (336.582kph), Bill Elliott (1987)	203.666 (325.866), Sterling Marlin (1987)	194.389 (311.022), Tommy Houston (1987)	N/A	200.209 (320.334), Bill Venturini (1987)	129.20 (206.72), Yannick Dalmas (1998)
Most Poles	Cale Yarborough, 4	Cale Yarborough, 8	Michael Waltrip, Donnie Allison, 3	N/A	Ferrell Harris, Benny Parsons, 3	N/A
Most Consecutive Poles	Bill Elliott, Ken Schrader, 3	Cale Yarborough, Sterling Marlin, Dale Earnhardt, 2	Frank Sechrist, Jack Ingram, 2	N/A	Benny Parsons, 3	N/A
Race Speed, mph (kph)	177.602 (284.163kph), Buddy Baker (1980)	173.473 (277.557), Bobby Allison (1980)	162.675 (260.28), Darrell Waltrip (1978)	187.793 (300.469), Dale Earnhardt (1996)	164.053 (262.489), Jack Bowsher (1966)	112.897 (180.635), Hasemi, Hoshino, Suzuki, and Oloffson (1992)
Most Wins	Richard Petty, 7	David Pearson, 5	Dale Earnhardt, 7	Dale Earnhardt, 5	Iggy Katona, 3	Hurley Haywood, 5
Most Consecutive Wins	Richard Petty, Cale Yarborough, Sterling Marlin, 2	David Pearson, 3	Dale Earnhardt, 5	Dale Earnhardt, 3	N/A	Peter Gregg, 3
Most Lead Changes	60 (1974)	49 (1974)	35 (1984, 1986)	25 (1997)	22 (1974)	N/A
Most Different Leaders	15 (1974, 1989, 1996)	14 (1986)	12 (1980)	8 (1976, 1997)	8 (1995)	N/A
Most Manufacturer Wins	Chevy, 14	Ford, 13	Chevy, 15	N/A	Chevy, 10	N/A
Lowest Starting Spot for a Winner	33rd, Bobby Allison	38th, Bill Elliott	42nd, Chad Little	12th, Rusty Wallace	30th, Iggy Katona	N/A

1959
Finish	Start	Car	Driver
1	15	42	Lee Petty
2	21	73	Johnny Beauchamp
3	17	18	Charley Griffith
4	11	6	Cotton Owens
5	7	48	Joe Weatherly
6	39	7	Jim Reed
7	41	47	Jack Smith
8	5	59	Tom Pistone
9	42	15	Tim Flock
10	31	1	Speedy Thompson

1960
Finish	Start	Car	Driver
1	9	27	Junior Johnson
2	4	3	Bobby Johns
3	19	43	Richard Petty
4	14	42	Lee Petty
5	11	69	Johnny Allen
6	54	11	Ned Jarrett
7	53	26	Curtis Turner
8	5	28	Fred Lorenzen
9	8	4	Rex White
10	15	85	Emanuel Zervakis

1961
Finish	Start	Car	Driver
1	4	20	Marvin Panch
2	2	8	Joe Weatherly
3	17	31	Paul Goldsmith
4	45	80	Fred Lorenzen
5	6	6	Cotton Owens
6	5	47	Jack Smith
7	9	11	Ned Jarrett
8	47	69	Johnny Allen
9	7	87	Buck Baker
10	18	59	Tom Pistone

1962
Finish	Start	Car	Driver
1	1	22	Fireball Roberts
2	10	43	Richard Petty
3	4	8	Joe Weatherly
4	3	47	Jack Smith
5	34	28	Fred Lorenzen
6	2	39	David Pearson
7	8	4	Rex White
8	35	94	Banjo Matthews
9	38	11	Ned Jarrett
10	17	44	Bob Welborn

1963
Finish	Start	Car	Driver
1	12	21	Tiny Lund
2	2	28	Fred Lorenzen
3	8	11	Ned Jarrett
4	10	29	Nelson Stacy
5	11	0	Dan Gurney
6	23	43	Richard Petty
7	14	7	Bobby Johns
8	26	8	Joe Weatherly
9	4	13	Johnny Rutherford
10	13	44	Tommy Irwin

1964
Finish	Start	Car	Driver
1	2	43	Richard Petty
2	6	54	Jim Pardue
3	1	25	Paul Goldsmith
4	9	21	Marvin Panch
5	10	5	Jim Paschal
6	21	1	Billy Wade
7	11	16	Darel Dieringer
8	14	23	Larry Frank
9	3	3	Junior Johnson
10	19	17	Dave McDonald

1965
Finish	Start	Car	Driver
1	4	28	Fred Lorenzen
2	1	16	Darel Dieringer
3	5	7	Bobby Johns
4	16	15	Earl Balmer
5	3	11	Ned Jarrett
6	6	21	Marvin Panch
7	28	29	Dick Hutcherson
8	10	24	Sam McQuagg
9	32	10	Cale Yarborough
10	36	49	G.C. Spencer

1966
Finish	Start	Car	Driver
1	1	43	Richard Petty
2	9	27	Cale Yarborough
3	12	6	David Pearson
4	9	28	Fred Lorenzen
5	11	98	Sam McQuagg
6	6	56	Jim Hurtubise
7	10	11	Ned Jarrett
8	8	12	LeeRoy Yarbrough
9	23	48	James Hylton
10	17	9	Larry Frank

1967
Finish	Start	Car	Driver
1	12	11	Mario Andretti
2	4	28	Fred Lorenzen
3	19	48	James Hylton
4	11	42	Tiny Lund
5	43	40	Jerry Grant
6	6	26	Darel Dieringer
7	18	90	Sonny Hutchings
8	2	43	Richard Petty
9	42	10	Jim Hurtubise
10	26	0	Neil Castles

1968
Finish	Start	Car	Driver
1	1	21	Cale Yarborough
2	3	26	LeeRoy Yarbrough
3	6	29	Bobby Allison
4	8	6	Al Unser
5	4	17	David Pearson
6	9	99	Paul Goldsmith
7	23	22	Darel Dieringer
8	2	43	Richard Petty
9	5	16	Tiny Lund
10	27	32	Andy Hampton

1969
Finish	Start	Car	Driver
1	19	98	LeeRoy Yarbrough
2	4	6	Charlie Glotzbach
3	7	27	Donnie Allison
4	9	11	A.J. Foyt
5	1	3	Buddy Baker
6	3	17	David Pearson
7	11	88	Benny Parsons
8	12	43	Richard Petty
9	50	58	Andy Hampton
10	16	96	Ray Elder

1970
Finish	Start	Car	Driver
1	9	40	Pete Hamilton
2	31	17	David Pearson
3	6	22	Bobby Allison
4	4	99	Charlie Glotzbach
5	3	71	Bobby Isaac
6	10	14	Richard Brickhouse
7	34	59	Jim Hurtubise
8	15	7	Ramo Stott
9	5	98	LeeRoy Yarbrough
10	33	30	Dave Marcis

1971
Finish	Start	Car	Driver
1	5	43	Richard Petty
2	6	11	Buddy Baker
3	1	21	A.J. Foyt
4	4	17	David Pearson
5	9	99	Fred Lorenzen
6	32	31	Jim Vandiver
7	8	22	Dick Brooks
8	24	20	Jim Hurtubise
9	15	48	James Hylton
10	2	71	Bobby Isaac

1972
Finish	Start	Car	Driver
1	2	21	A.J. Foyt
2	6	6	Charlie Glotzbach
3	8	31	Jim Vandiver
4	33	72	Benny Parsons
5	35	48	James Hylton
6	16	3	Cale Yarborough
7	23	5	David Sisco
8	21	25	Jabe Thomas
9	15	4	John Sears
10	13	23	Vic Elford

1973
Finish	Start	Car	Driver
1	7	43	Richard Petty
2	10	15	Bobby Isaac
3	9	6	Dick Brooks
4	8	50	A.J. Foyt
5	6	4	Herschel McGriff
6	1	71	Buddy Baker
7	12	48	James Hylton
8	16	90	Ramo Stott
9	36	67	Buddy Arrington
10	27	45	Vic Parsons

1974

Finish	Start	Car	Driver
1	2	43	Richard Petty
2	4	11	Cale Yarborough
3	12	83	Ramo Stott
4	31	14	Coo Coo Marlin
5	35	50	A.J. Foyt
6	7	88	Donnie Allison
7	11	95	Darrell Waltrip
8	3	27	Bobby Isaac
9	23	32	Dick Brooks
10	18	30	Walter Ballard

1975

Finish	Start	Car	Driver
1	32	72	Benny Parsons
2	3	16	Bobby Allison
3	6	11	Cale Yarborough
4	2	21	David Pearson
5	31	83	Ramo Stott
6	8	71	Dave Marcis
7	4	43	Richard Petty
8	10	98	Ritchie Panch
9	37	49	G.C. Spencer
10	17	48	James Hylton

1976

Finish	Start	Car	Driver
1	7	21	David Pearson
2	6	43	Richard Petty
3	32	72	Benny Parsons
4	11	54	Lennie Pond
5	13	12	Neil Bonnett
6	2	81	Terry Ryan
7	41	70	J.D. McDuffie
8	19	63	Terry Blivins
9	36	3	Richard Childress
10	34	79	Frank Warren

1977

Finish	Start	Car	Driver
1	4	11	Cale Yarborough
2	6	72	Benny Parsons
3	8	15	Buddy Baker
4	13	14	Coo Coo Marlin
5	15	90	Dick Brooks
6	2	51	A.J. Foyt
7	10	88	Darrell Waltrip
8	23	52	Jimmy Means
9	30	19	Ron Burcham
10	37	48	James Hylton

1978

Finish	Start	Car	Driver
1	33	15	Bobby Allison
2	1	11	Cale Yarborough
3	8	72	Benny Parsons
4	2	53	Ron Hutcherson
5	32	90	Dick Brooks
6	10	2	Dave Marcis
7	31	27	Buddy Baker
8	9	9	Bill Elliott
9	23	6	Ferrel Harris
10	28	54	Lennie Pond

1979

Finish	Start	Car	Driver
1	13	43	Richard Petty
2	4	88	Darrell Waltrip
3	6	51	A.J. Foyt
4	2	1	Donnie Allison
5	3	11	Cale Yarborough
6	33	30	Tighe Scott
7	28	68	Chuck Bown
8	10	2	Dale Earnhardt
9	37	14	Coo Coo Marlin
10	24	79	Frank Warren

1980

Finish	Start	Car	Driver
1	1	28	Buddy Baker
2	9	15	Bobby Allison
3	3	21	Neil Bonnett
4	32	2	Dale Earnhardt
5	14	27	Benny Parsons
6	17	44	Terry Labonte
7	2	1	Donnie Allison
8	36	14	Sterling Marlin
9	12	75	Lennie Pond
10	27	90	Jody Ridley

1981

Finish	Start	Car	Driver
1	8	43	Richard Petty
2	1	28	Bobby Allison
3	5	88	Ricky Rudd
4	6	1	Buddy Baker
5	7	2	Dale Earnhardt
6	16	9	Bill Elliott
7	27	90	Jody Ridley
8	29	27	Cale Yarborough
9	34	75	Joe Milikan
10	35	98	Johnny Rutherford

1982

Finish	Start	Car	Driver
1	7	88	Bobby Allison
2	3	27	Cale Yarborough
3	8	2	Joe Ruttman
4	5	44	Terry Labonte
5	20	9	Bill Elliott
6	22	47	Ron Bouchard
7	2	33	Harry Gant
8	4	1	Buddy Baker
9	23	90	Jody Ridley
10	38	30	Roy Smith

1983

Finish	Start	Car	Driver
1	8	28	Cale Yarborough
2	17	9	Bill Elliott
3	5	21	Buddy Baker
4	11	98	Joe Ruttman
5	10	90	Dick Brooks
6	41	44	Terry Labonte
7	22	53	Tom Sneva
8	15	16	David Pearson
9	35	22	Bobby Allison
10	18	84	Jody Ridley

1984

Finish	Start	Car	Driver
1	1	28	Cale Yarborough
2	29	3	Dale Earnhardt
3	26	11	Darrell Waltrip
4	7	12	Neil Bonnett
5	3	9	Bill Elliott
6	6	33	Harry Gant
7	14	15	Ricky Rudd
8	9	5	Geoff Bodine
9	11	16	David Pearson
10	33	84	Jody Ridley

1985

Finish	Start	Car	Driver
1	1	9	Bill Elliott
2	14	75	Lake Speed
3	3	11	Darrell Waltrip
4	7	88	Buddy Baker
5	9	15	Ricky Rudd
6	13	51	Greg Sacks
7	17	5	Geoff Bodine
8	22	2	Rusty Wallace
9	38	8	Bobby Hillin Jr.
10	19	12	Neil Bonnett

1986

Finish	Start	Car	Driver
1	2	5	Geoff Bodine
2	5	44	Terry Labonte
3	6	11	Darrell Waltrip
4	25	8	Bobby Hillin Jr.
5	31	55	Benny Parsons
6	14	98	Ron Bouchard
7	16	4	Rick Wilson
8	9	27	Rusty Wallace
9	8	1	Sterling Marlin
10	36	75	Lake Speed

1987

Finish	Start	Car	Driver
1	1	9	Bill Elliott
2	4	35	Benny Parsons
3	11	43	Richard Petty
4	7	88	Buddy Baker
5	13	3	Dale Earnhardt
6	6	22	Bobby Allison
7	3	90	Ken Schrader
8	5	17	Darrell Waltrip
9	31	15	Ricky Rudd
10	22	29	Cale Yarborough

1988

Finish	Start	Car	Driver
1	3	12	Bobby Allison
2	2	28	Davey Allison
3	19	55	Phil Parsons
4	14	75	Neil Bonnett
5	8	11	Terry Labonte
6	1	25	Ken Schrader
7	5	27	Rusty Wallace
8	12	44	Sterling Marlin
9	18	88	Buddy Baker
10	6	3	Dale Earnhardt

1989

Finish	Start	Car	Driver
1	2	17	Darrell Waltrip
2	1	25	Ken Schrader
3	8	3	Dale Earnhardt
4	10	5	Geoff Bodine
5	7	55	Phil Parsons
6	11	66	Rick Mast
7	9	7	Alan Kulwicki
8	40	4	Rick Wilson
9	4	11	Terry Labonte
10	41	23	Eddie Bierschwale

1990

Finish	Start	Car	Driver
1	12	10	Derrike Cope
2	20	1	Terry Labonte
3	4	9	Bill Elliott
4	19	5	Ricky Rudd
5	2	3	Dale Earnhardt
6	10	8	Bobby Hillin Jr.
7	38	27	Rusty Wallace
8	24	30	Michael Waltrip
9	3	11	Geoff Bodine
10	30	15	Morgan Shepherd

1991

Finish	Start	Car	Driver
1	2	4	Ernie Irvan
2	12	22	Sterling Marlin
3	14	75	Joe Ruttman
4	7	1	Rick Mast
5	4	3	Dale Earnhardt
6	17	21	Dale Jarrett
7	36	27	Bobby Hillin Jr.
8	27	7	Alan Kulwicki
9	9	5	Ricky Rudd
10	20	68	Bobby Hamilton

1992

Finish	Start	Car	Driver
1	6	28	Davey Allison
2	4	21	Morgan Shepherd
3	16	15	Geoff Bodine
4	41	7	Alan Kulwicki
5	28	75	Dick Trickle
6	33	42	Kyle Petty
7	34	94	Terry Labonte
8	40	55	Ted Musgrave
9	3	3	Dale Earnhardt
10	19	9	Phil Parsons

1993

Finish	Start	Car	Driver
1	2	18	Dale Jarrett
2	4	3	Dale Earnhardt
3	6	15	Geoff Bodine
4	16	27	Hut Stricklin
5	3	24	Jeff Gordon
6	23	6	Mark Martin
7	32	21	Morgan Shepherd
8	7	25	Ken Schrader
9	14	8	Sterling Marlin
10	22	16	Wally Dallenbach

1994

Finish	Start	Car	Driver
1	4	4	Sterling Marlin
2	3	28	Ernie Irvan
3	9	5	Terry Labonte
4	6	24	Jeff Gordon
5	12	21	Morgan Shepherd
6	31	77	Greg Sacks
7	2	3	Dale Earnhardt
8	20	10	Ricky Rudd
9	8	11	Bill Elliott
10	13	25	Ken Schrader

1995

Finish	Start	Car	Driver
1	3	4	Sterling Marlin
2	2	3	Dale Earnhardt
3	6	6	Mark Martin
4	12	16	Ted Musgrave
5	1	28	Dale Jarrett
6	15	30	Michael Waltrip
7	35	29	Steve Grissom
8	11	5	Terry Labonte
9	9	25	Ken Schrader
10	30	21	Morgan Shepherd

1996

Finish	Start	Car	Driver
1	7	88	Dale Jarrett
2	1	3	Dale Earnhardt
3	4	25	Ken Schrader
4	15	6	Mark Martin
5	16	99	Jeff Burton
6	9	15	Wally Dallenbach
7	20	16	Ted Musgrave
8	21	94	Bill Elliott
9	10	10	Ricky Rudd
10	11	21	Michael Waltrip

1997

Finish	Start	Car	Driver
1	6	24	Jeff Gordon
2	18	5	Terry Labonte
3	40	25	Ricky Craven
4	8	94	Bill Elliott
5	9	4	Sterling Marlin
6	21	37	Jeremy Mayfield
7	11	6	Mark Martin
8	17	22	Ward Burton
9	13	10	Ricky Rudd
10	22	17	Darrell Waltrip

1998

Finish	Start	Car	Driver
1	4	3	Dale Earnhardt
2	1	18	Bobby Labonte
3	13	12	Jeremy Mayfield
4	31	25	Ken Schrader
5	12	2	Rusty Wallace
6	10	42	Ernie Irvan
7	21	97	Chad Little
8	8	31	Mike Skinner
9	6	21	Michael Waltrip
10	19	94	Bill Elliott

1999

Finish	Start	Car	Driver
1	1	24	Jeff Gordon
2	4	3	Dale Earnhardt
3	41	28	Kenny Irwin
4	12	31	Mike Skinner
5	13	7	Michael Waltrip
6	7	33	Ken Schrader
7	24	44	Kyle Petty
8	10	2	Rusty Wallace
9	26	97	Chad Little
10	21	98	Rick Mast

2000

Finish	Start	Car	Driver
1	1	88	Dale Jarrett
2	14	99	Jeff Burton
3	3	94	Bill Elliott
4	5	2	Rusty Wallace
5	9	6	Mark Martin
6	13	18	Bobby Labonte
7	25	5	Terry Labonte
8	6	22	Ward Burton
9	23	36	Ken Schrader
10	34	17	Matt Kenseth

2001

Finish	Start	Car	Driver
1	19	15	Michael Waltrip
2	6	8	Dale Earnhardt Jr.
3	12	2	Rusty Wallace
4	30	28	Ricky Rudd
5	1	9	Bill Elliott
6	27	7	Mike Wallace
7	3	40	Sterling Marlin
8	34	55	Bobby Hamilton
9	42	12	Jeremy Mayfield
10	2	92	Stacy Compton

Photo Credits

Allsport: ©**Jonathan Ferry:** pp. 118–119, 135; ©**Robert Laberge:** p. 136; ©**Jamie Squire:** pp. 6–7, 9 right, 130–131, 132–133, 134 bottom, 138, 140–141, 143, 147, 149; ©**David Taylor:** pp. 2–3, 91 right, 110–111, 112, 127 bottom, 128–129, 131 right; ©**Jim Gund:** pp. 103 top, 106 inset; ©**Steve Swope:** p. 108; ©**Andy Lyons:** pp. 114 inset, 120, 148

©**AP/Wide World Photos:** pp. 24 top, 28–29, 37, 40–41, 52 bottom, 63, 117 bottom, 122, 123

Archive Photos: ©**Terry Atwell:** p. 124 top

Brown Brothers: pp. 13 bottom, 14 top, 14 bottom, 15, 16–17, 17 top

Corbis: pp. 20 bottom, 25, 26–27, 29 top right, 36, 39, 40 bottom, 43, 46, 48 top, 49, 50 bottom, 53 top, 57 top, 59, 68, 69, 71 right, 72, 74 left, 85, 87 top right, 87 bottom right, 88 left, 99, 117 top, 134 top, 137 top, 139, 146

Icon Sports Media: ©**Jim Gund:** pp. 113, 114 top, 127 top

International Motorsports Hall of Fame: pp. 10–11, 13 top, 19 bottom, 22–23, 23 inset, 24 bottom, 30 top, 30 bottom, 32, 35 right, 38, 42 bottom, 45 top, 55 right, 58 inset, 61 top, 61 bottom, 62, 66, 119 right

©**ISC/Daytona Archives:** pp. 12, 20 top, 21, 22 left, 29 bottom, 31 top left, 65 right, 76, 79, 80 inset, 83 inset, 97 right, 116, 124 bottom

©**Nigel Kinrade:** pp. 90–91, 125 bottom

©**Al Messerschmidt:** pp. 115, 121

Dozier Mobley Collection: pp. 5, 54–55, 56, 57 bottom, 60, 64–65, 67, 74–75, 78 bottom, 82, 83 bottom, 86–87, 88-89, 92 left

Courtesy **National Speed Sport News:** pp: 47, 48 bottom, 51 top, 58 bottom; ©**Chris Economaki:** pp. 34–35, 53 bottom; ©**Ray Fenn:** p. 45 bottom; ©**C.V. Haschell:** pp. 42 top, 50 top

©**Dorsey Patrick:** pp. 70–71, 73, 77 top, 77 bottom, 78 top, 80 bottom, 81, 84

©**Joe Robbins:** pp. 8–9, 142, 144–145, endpapers

Larry Shurter Collection: pp. 31 right, 33 top, 33 bottom left, 33 bottom right

©**Mike Slade:** pp. 51 bottom, 52 top, 92–93, 93 top, 94–95, 96–97, 101 top, 101 bottom, 102

Sports Chrome: ©**Ron McQueeny:** p. 103 bottom; ©**Brian Spurlock:** p. 137 bottom; ©**Greg Crisp:** pp. 98, 100, 105, 106–107, 125 top; ©**Evan Pinkus:** pp. 150–151

©**Steve Swope:** pp. 104, 109

Underwood Archives: pp. 16 top, 18, 19 top

©**P. Webb:** p. 126

Digital Imaging: Daniel J. Rutkowski

Index